Dard & Ribo, M & P Benetière, Bruno Duchène, J.F Nicq, Noune,
Laurent Cazottes, Johny Halliday, Blandine Chauchat, Philippe Pacalet,
Philippe Wies, Leon Barral, Marcel Lapierre, Catherine & Pierre Breton
Anthony Tortul, Loïc Roure, Stephane Morin, Michel Guignier, Pon pon,
N & C Chaussart, Michel Favard, A & C Binner, Antoine Arena, Yvon Métras
Ludwig Bindernagel, Gregory Leclerc, Toby Bainbridge, Thierry Michon
Anselm Selosse, Jacques Lassaigne, Philippe Botex, Jean Christophe Garnier
J.F Ganevat, Sarnin Berux, Sebastien Riffault, Alexandre Bain,
Philippe Valette, Thierry Puzelat, Pierre Overnoy, Richard Leroy,
D & P. Belluard, Nicolas Réal, Jean Claude Rateau, Nicolas Carmarans,
Noëlla Morantin, Hervé Villemade, Laurent Lebled, Mathieu Barret
Sebastien Bobinet, Luc Sebille, Jean Sebastien Gioan, Graven'er,
Frank Cornelissen, Ariana Occhipinti, Canzòn, Hatzidakis
Olivier Rivière, Lise & Bertrand Jousset, Angeline Mauch, Favovino
Gulio Armani, Julien Frémont, Cyril Zangs, Xavier Caillard ...

Eating with the Chefs

pp. 2–3: Le Chateaubriand, Paris, France
        (see pp. 118–33)

pp. 4–5: Royal Mail, Dunkeld, Victoria,
        Australia (see pp. 262–77)

pp. 6–7: Maison Pic, Valence, France
        (see pp. 150–65)

p. 8:   Quay, Sydney, Australia
        (see pp. 230–45)

p. 21: wd-50, New York City, USA
        (see pp. 294–309)

Eating with the Chefs

Family meals from the world's
most creative restaurants

Per-Anders Jörgensen

Introduction

As a documentary photographer the most important thing for me has always been the human story. This project has been particularly fascinating because it is a window into a hidden side of the people who make the restaurant industry happen. To capture staff preparing and eating their own "family meal," whether they do it standing up at their station, in the debris of the dining room after service, or in the shade of a tree in a beautiful garden, gives a very human perspective on how they think about and relate to food. The good-natured banter and teasing, blazing discussions on soccer and politics, tales of life and love, is a mirror of how we come together as societies. It also tells you a lot about what makes a restaurant tick.

Restaurants have always been important to me, as practical places where you go to get fed, but also as marker destinations where you come to celebrate so many events in your life. I grew up in Ystad in Southern Sweden in the 1970s, and because my parents were hard-workers I often went to a local restaurant for my supper. I could often be found there, dining on my favorite meal of a steak and fries washed down with a bottle of coke. My fellow diners probably found the sight of this young boy eating alone a bit awkward, but for me it was heaven, because my family meal was right there, among the staff and chefs that worked there.

This early experience of a different kind of "family meal" sowed the seed for the creation of *Eating with the Chefs,* although the idea didn't really start to take shape until ten years ago. I had just finished a shoot at Mugaritz near San Sebastián in the north of Spain and was hanging out with the staff and Chef Andoni Luis Aduriz after lunch service. It was a lot less international and a lot more rustic back then—staff meal in fact was served in what would later become the lab—but I do remember being struck by the huge contrast between what they served in the dining room and what they fed themselves. It was solid, Basque peasant food—bean stews, hearty rice dishes, pork ribs— the kind of food that I knew Andoni's mother would have cooked. I was struck by the notion that so many restaurants must be mirroring family life like this backstage in their kitchens, and cooking the kind of honest, simple food that if you're lucky you have at home. That's something there is far too little of in the world today.

Staff meals have not always been something to be proud of. Most chefs have horror stories to share about what they have been fed in restaurants ranging from scrag ends of meat to nothing at all. But the mind-set has changed dramatically over the past decade with more and more focus being placed on the way staff are fed and looked after. It has become so important

that cooking schools and catering colleges, such as the International
Culinary Center in New York City, have added it to the curriculum,
now dedicating a month to teaching students how to cook and budget
for staff meals.

I found it incredibly humbling to see first hand the kind of brute-hard
work that goes into creating a restaurant at this level, and it made me realize
that we cannot take these places for granted. This very intimate, behind-the-
scenes portrait of some of the world's most interesting restaurants is my way
of celebrating and honoring them. Those included have been chosen based
on the people and places I have got to know and love over the years, and who
have broken new ground in what they do. Eventually, I narrowed the scope
down to 18 very different places scattered all over the world, but there are so
many other places that are just as worthy of this recognition and this is for
them too. What they all have in common is the importance they place on staff
meal, not just as a means of nourishment, but as a tool for building a successful
culture and business.

The 21st-century staff meal has multiple roles that go way beyond
keeping people alive. It is essential for morale, and perhaps most importantly,
for promoting a sense of belonging, whether you're washing dishes, a line
cook or a sous chef: the glue that cements the team together. In Southern
Europe, for example, it is like being part of a big, extended family with the
entire team sitting down to eat together at the same time. When you go to
other parts of the world, where family values are no longer quite so prevalent
in society, many staff will eat standing up. But no matter how you eat it,
wherever the family meal is deeply rooted in the culture of the restaurant, you
find a business that is thriving and a staff who are happy.

The big question when I started this book was how do you feed so
many people food that is fresh, good, and cheap enough each day to make
it work for the business? The answer lay in how it gets paid back. At Noma in
Copenhagen, where people have come to do their stagiaire from every corner
of the world, they often use the staff meal as a way of showcasing the food of
their home country. Consequently, they understand each other better and are
much more powerful as a team. Chef Paolo Lopriore at Il Canto, Siena, insists
on cooking the staff meal himself as a way of showing how much he appreciates
his staff and his team, in turn, work with an almost unbridled passion. At
restaurants like Le Chateaubriand in Paris, someone will simply open the
walk-in refrigerator and seize the opportunity to cook with what is available.
New ideas are born every day. And for aspiring chefs like Sunny, a dishwasher I

met at Attica in Melbourne, it's a chance to show off their own skills at the stove—a perk that head chef Ben Shewry is actively promoting—while spreading an important message: anything and everything is possible.

There is no doubt in my mind that restaurants benefit hugely from teams that are firing at 110 percent at all times. What is interesting is how it affects the team. Pride is a powerful thing and it seems that when they cook for each other that sense of pride swells in a way that is very similar to parents coaching their children, or friendly rivalry between brothers and sisters. This positive energy in the kitchen ripples out to anyone sitting in the dining room. You can literally taste it.

This book has gone full circle. The contents not only document the evolution and future of staff meals in restaurants, but offer a glimpse of the future of casual dining. It will not be long before the staff meal moves out of professional kitchens and becomes the theme of the restaurant itself.

It is no surprise that the family meal has evolved to become an extension of why people work in restaurants in the first place. Now more than ever it is fundamental to their success, and symbolic of what makes a good restaurant great.

Per-Anders Jörgensen

Think like a chef. Cook like a chef.

Modern cooking has become a serious art, but it is also something very instinctive. Ask any of the chefs in this book how they approach their craft and they all have one thing in common: to use recipes as guidelines and inspiration rather than law. While some restaurants of course are very technical and scientific, the fundamental mind-set is to be open, exploratory, and unencumbered by rules. At its most basic level this is especially true when cooking the "family meal," and it is especially relevant to home cooks. The act of cooking should be free-form and open-ended, a journey as much as a destination.

Like any skill, having a core knowledge of the basics is a solid foundation for creating something good, but adapting the guidelines and making these dishes your own will make the act of cooking a lot more rewarding. Use the best ingredients you can afford, seek out products that are in season, and resist the temptation to manipulate them too much. It sounds obvious, but it goes much deeper than that. If you get into the habit of building relationships with the ingredients themselves, you'll get much more out of them. "Here we say you're not just peeling asparagus," says Julieta Caruso, chef de cuisine at Mugaritz. "You're connected to it—from the moment it is picked and taken to the kitchen, until it is dressed and plated."

Chef Michael Gallina, chef de cuisine at Blue Hill at Stone Barns, lives by the rule that if it's edible there's a use for it. "Nothing should go in the garbage," he says. If you cook from the premise that trimmings from every cut of meat, fruit, or vegetable can be used as the base for soups and stocks, not only will your weekly shop go much farther, but no matter how simple the dish, the flavors will soar. Agata Felluga, sous chef at Le Chateaubriand is a master of leftovers. "If you get to the end of the week and all you have left is half an onion, a lemon, and a pumpkin, roast them all together and turn them into soup or a puree. It's amazing what you can get out of nothing, so think of recipes like maps. It's a way of getting from A to B, but that doesn't mean you have to obey them."

Learning some basic techniques like how to balance salt, acidity, fat, and sweetness allows for improvisation with anything that falls into those categories. For example, if a dish calls for a teaspoonful of vinegar, a squeeze of lemon juice can often be just as powerful as long as you understand the role acid plays in balancing flavors. The same applies to just about any ingredient you can think of. "Herbs cause a lot of confusion," says Peter Gunn, junior sous chef at Attica, "But as a general rule you can substitute a soft herb with a soft herb, such as parsley for cilantro (coriander), mint for basil,

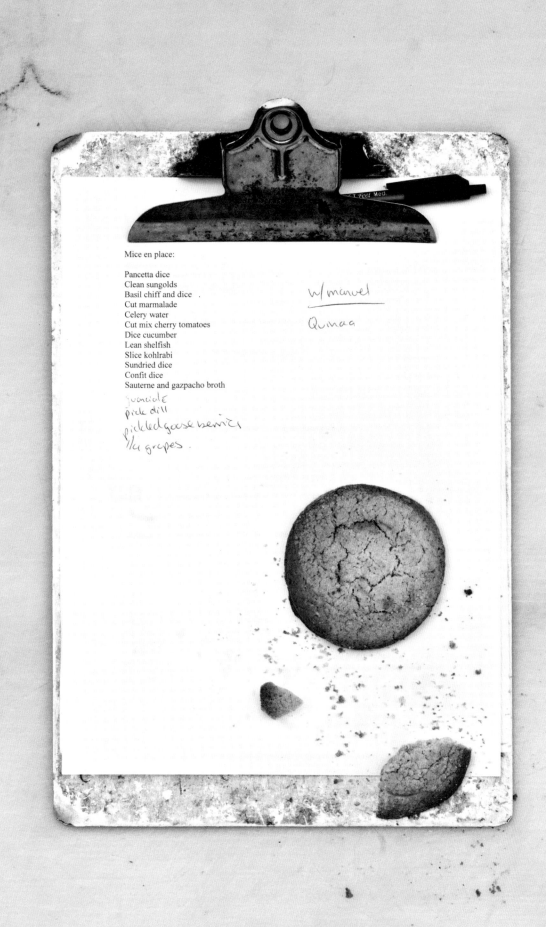

Mice en place:

Pancetta dice
Clean sungolds
Basil chiff and dice .
Cut marmalade
Celery water
Cut mix cherry tomatoes
Dice cucumber
Lean shelfish
Slice kohlrabi
Sundried dice
Confit dice
Sauterne and gazpacho broth
guanciole
pick dill
pickled gooseberries
1/4 grapes .

w/ marvel

Quinaa

chervil for tarragon, and woody herbs for woody herbs—rosemary for thyme, oregano for sage, marjoram for bay. What you usually can't do is replace woody herbs with soft. Rosemary in place of parsley just doesn't work." You won't get exactly the same flavor as the dish in the recipe, but you'll get something that works, possibly something that's even better and it's yours.

A willingness to explore and having a great sense of adventure nudges you still closer to the workings of a chef's mind. Food doesn't just happen in the kitchen, you need to search it out in local markets and specialty stores, taste things you've never seen before and buy whatever looks good rather than what a recipe necessarily for calls for. If the eggplants (aubergines) are squashy use zucchini (courgettes), if the lamb looks gray, choose a fat organic chicken, if the fish looks tired, maybe seafood would do? Nearly everything can be reappropriated. "Let the seasons tell you where to begin," advises Gallina. "I go to a farmers market with no idea of what I'm going to cook and get inspired from there. The trick is to let the best ingredients lead the way."

Having a pantry stock cupboard filled with "secret" ingredients will also give your cooking an edge. Essentials like nut and olive oils or vinegars, can be given a flavor boost by adding orange or lemon peel, chiles or garlic, herbs and spices, and just one pickle or preserve recipe can be applied to pretty much any fruit or vegetable. These small adjustments to a base product allow you to make a recipe your own, and ensures you always have something interesting to bring to a dressing or to liven up a plate of cheese or charcuterie. Similarly, your local Japanese or Asian food store is likely to have a more interesting range of noodles than a supermarket that only stocks a generic brand.

Like most things in life, practice makes perfect, but it's better to have a handful of things you do really well and are comfortable with than a lot of things you do poorly. The fundamental French tradition of mise en place— literally getting everything prepped and ready before you start cooking— is the key to being successful at just about anything. Background reading, not just recipe books but food books generally, provides inspiration but also helps to put things into context and create your own "food memory." "I read lots of old recipe books for the literature and history of a dish," says Felluga, "Ferran Adrià once said something that really made an impression on me. He said, you should record your own recipes whether you're cooking at home or working professionally, because that is where you best learn from the failures and the successes." It's fair to say many of the world's greatest dishes have come about that way.

Asador Etxebarri

Location
Atxondo, Bizkaia, Spain

Established
1990

Head chef
Victor Arguinzoniz

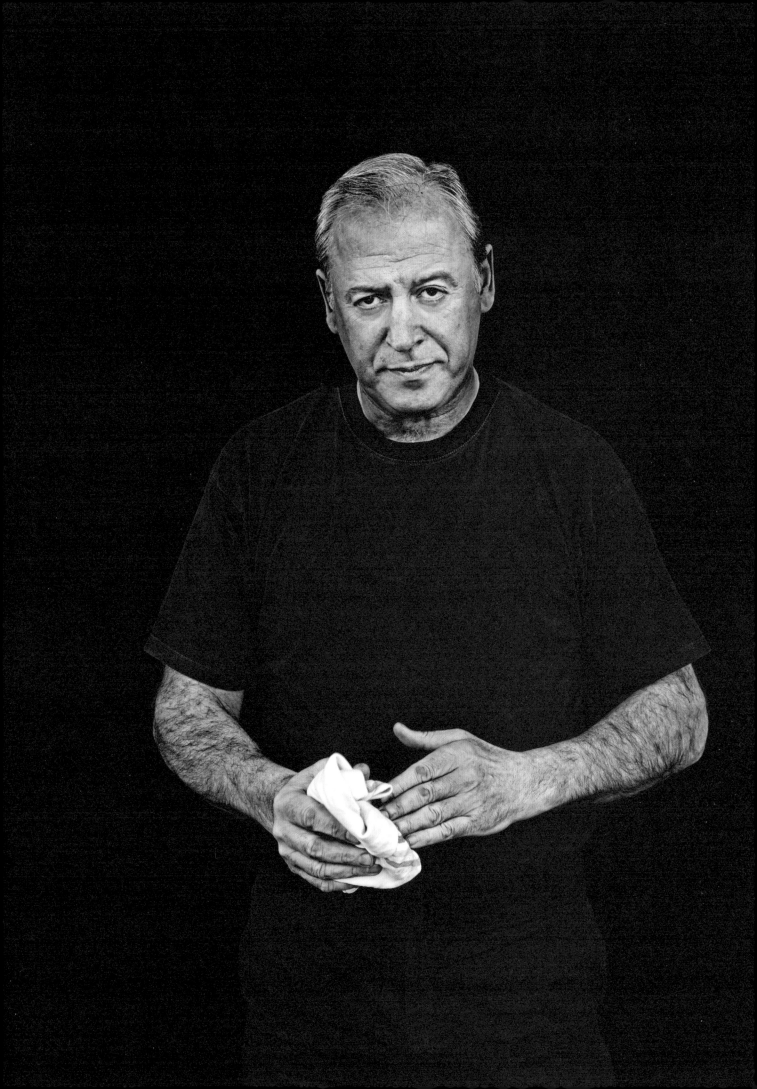

← Winter vegetables are stored outside in the mountain's natural refrigerator.

↑ Staff enjoy dishes that are always familiar, homely, and delicious (top and above).

→ The essence of Etxebarri's staff meal: hearty and very frugal.

↑ Home made chorizo with eggs, a rare treat
at Etxebarri.

Asador Etxebarri

There is an unwritten rule at Asador Etxebarri that when you cook staff meal, no matter where you come from, you can only do grandma's cooking. "The most important thing is to do something that is true to the region," owner-chef Victor says, "It should be familiar, homely and delicious." His sentiment completely fits with this remote little restaurant where a strong emotional attachment to the "old" way is a powerful driver for the new.

Arriving in this tiny little village in the Basque foothills with its miniature church and huge pelota (a Basque bat-and-ball game) court, where the only sounds to be heard are the dunk, dunk, dunk of the pelota and the bongling of sheep bells, it feels only half awake, which is exactly your first impression on entering Etxebarri. The street-level floor is unremarkable, a traditional bar with a long wooden bar, dark wooden furniture, and hard benches. It's where the old women of the village come to play cards, and where the local mailman stops for his morning glass of brandy, but upstairs you enter a completely different world of Spanish fine dining.

The place has changed immeasurably over the past few years, going from old-fashioned chop-house to destination restaurant with all that brings—stagiaires clamoring to get in, media attention, Michelin inspectors—but their daily meal has always remained the same. It helps those who work here understand the contrasts of the culture and establishing a strong connection to the region through its dishes is essential, to the extent that they will even spend two days making something like *morros y callos*—a hearty dish of face and tripe stewed down with onion, garlic, and red bell peppers for eight hours and served the next day.

"Our staff meal is very strong food and very frugal," says Eneko Diaz, who has been cooking it for the last nine years. "It's the kind of food we eat at home and when I compare it to working on the pastry station, which is very precise, to me it represents freedom."

As is traditional in Spain, once a year after the *matanza* (the pig slaughter) Victor makes the mother of all chorizos to last the rest of the year, and every now and then, he makes his staff *choripan*. Slicing the sausages down the middle he places them directly on top of the glowing red coals in a hinged grill. It allows the meat to caramelize instead of burn, and served hot and juicy between two slices of rustic, country bread it is the ultimate treat. An edible memory of a Basque childhood, and like everything served for staff meal, it has the kind of old school familiarity that is reassuringly grounding in the fast changing world of fine dining.

Basque-Style Garlic Soup

→ p. 33

1   Put the olive oil into a saucepan. Add the onions and cook over medium heat until soft, stirring occasionally. Add the garlic, turn the heat to low, and cook until golden brown while stirring.

2   Stir in the paprika and cook for one minute more.

3   Add the bread, red peppers, and water. Cook at a low simmer until the bread has almost dissolved and a thick soup has formed.

4   Serve in warmed bowls topped with the slices of jamon.

	for 2	for 6	for 20	for 50
olive oil	–	2 tbsp	6 tbsp	1 cup/250 ml
red onions, thinly sliced	–	1	3	7
heads of garlic, crushed	–	1	3	7
paprika	–	1 tbsp	3 tbsp	7 tbsp
stale baguette, cut into bits	–	½	1½	4
dried red peppers (*choricero*)	–	3	9	22
water	–	8½ cups/2 L	20 cups/5 L	12 qt/11.5 L
slices of jamon (dry-cured ham)	–	6	20	50

Tripe and Nose à la Vizcaína

→ p. 34
Begin preparation 1 day before serving

1 Wash the tripe and nose carefully. To clean the tripe thoroughly, scrub it with sea salt and water as if you were cleaning clothes. Remove and discard any dark parts. Cut into bite-size pieces. Put into a large saucepan and cover with cold water. Bring to a boil, then remove the tripe from the water and repeat this process. Follow the same process for the nose. Remember to clean it well to be sure that the flavor is not too overpowering. Keep both sets of cooking water.

2 After the tripe and nose have been blanched twice, put into a saucepan along with the onion, garlic, carrots, parsley, and salt. Cover with cold water and bring to a gentle simmer. Cook for 2 hours or until the tripe and nose are tender.

3 Make the salsa. Soak the red peppers in warm water for 30 minutes.

4 Put the olive oil in a large skillet or frying pan. Add the onions and cook over medium-low heat until softened, stirring frequently.

5 Add the bread and pancetta. Continue to cook until golden.

6 Add the drained peppers and fry the whole mixture gently until it resembles a thick paste. Add the cooking water from the tripe, then pass through a vegetable mill twice or process in the food processor until smooth. If it seems too thick add more water.

7 Place the salsa in a saucepan. Add the tripe and nose to the salsa. Bring to a boil, then let cool to room temperature. Refrigerate for 1 day before serving to let the flavors to blend. Reheat to serve.

for the tripe	for 2	for 6	for 20	for 50
honeycomb tripe	1 lb/450 g	2½ lb/1.2 kg	7½ lb/3.6 kg	–
nose of a cow	¼	½	2	–
white onions, sliced	1 small	1	3	–
heads of garlic	¼	½	2	–
carrots, sliced	½ small	1 small	3	–
sprigs parsley	2	6	12	–
sea salt	to taste	to taste	to taste	–

for the salsa	for 2	for 6	for 20	for 50
dried romano red peppers, seeded and chopped	4	12	36	–
olive oil	2 tsp	2 tbsp	6 tbsp	–
red onions, thinly sliced	1	3	9	–
white onions, thinly sliced	1	3	9	–
slices of bread, torn into pieces	1 small	1	3	–
slice of pancetta, chopped	½	½	2	–

Basque-Style Junket

→ p. 35

1   At the restaurant, a red hot poker is inserted into the milk to give it the traditional toasted flavor. (Alternatively, heat the milk to the steaming point then let cool to 110°F/40°C.)

2   Crush the rennet tablet and stir into the water to dissolve. Stir into the hot milk.

3   Strain into ramekins and let stand for 10 minutes.

4   Place the junket in the refrigerator to chill for at least 4 hours or overnight. Serve in the individual ramekins accompanied by the honey.

	for 2	for 6	for 20	for 50
sheep milk	1⅓ cups/325 ml	4 cups/950 ml	10 cups/2.4 L	–
rennet	⅓ tablet	1 tablet	2½ tablets	–
water	1 tsp	1 tbsp	2½ tbsp	–
honey	4 tsp	4 tbsp	10 tbsp	–

↑ Basque-Style Garlic Soup (p. 30).

Asador Etxebarri

↑ Tripe and Nose à la Vizcaína (p. 31). → Basque-Style Junket (p. 32). → Parque Natural de Urkiola (overleaf).

Attica

Location
Melbourne, Australia

Established
2003

Head chef
Ben Shewry

Senior sous chef
James Snelleman

Junior sous chef
Peter Gunn

← From left to right: Peter Gunn, James Snelleman, Mo Zhou, Matthew Boyle, Lorcan Kan, Pascale Beirouti, and Ben Shewry gather around Lorcan Mulhern's Astroturf covered car of "life" (previous page).

← Peter Gunn and James Snelleman treat short ribs to long, slow cooking.

↑ Dustbusters—in a small team, all jobs are shared and given equal importance.

→ The makings of Australian Tom Yum (p. 46), (overleaf).

Attica

The restaurant world is full of visionaries, among them Ben Shewry, head chef at Melbourne's Attica and the brains behind a tour de force known not so much for flashy techniques as for its ability to stir your soul.

Ben grew up in a remote part of New Zealand where gardening and foraging were the norm. When he opened Attica, he wanted to create contemporary food that provoked memories, evoked emotions, and expressed the environment of both Australia and New Zealand by shining a light on less celebrated ingredients and on the talents of bright new chefs. His signature dish of "potatoes cooked in soil" was something he picked up from Maori cooks in New Zealand who use earthen ovens.

The staff meal is inseparable from that idea, starting with dishes of extreme freshness inspired by the team's collective memories with a strong emotional kick. While the dishes themselves may span several countries and cultures, the backbone comes from foraged sea vegetables and shellfish, exotic meats, such as wallaby, and unusual Aboriginal sources of food, such as the giant pine nuts that grow naturally on the Ripponlea Estate, where Attica also has its vegetable gardens. Sous chef Peter Gunn, in charge of the gardens, describes gardening time as valuable "head space."

They have turned the parking lot behind the restaurant into a herb garden, smokery, and bread oven, which gives plenty of scope for experimenting, an ethos that runs deep in Ben's philosophy of food. If his own dishes are highly personal, he's magnificently open in encouraging his staff to dig deep into food that triggers memories of their own.

Like a culinary philanthropist, Ben provides opportunity where he sees potential. Sunny started out as a dishwasher, but began cooking his mother's Indian food—chicken curry, daal, raita, and homemade parathas—when it was his turn to do the staff meal. "You can get Indian food in restaurants, but it is not actual Indian food because it mixed with all kinds of preservatives and colors," he explains. "By adding all that, we are playing with the taste and not making the food healthy. I like to make real Indian food, and in this manner I can let people know the taste of actual India."

Sunny has since been promoted to junior chef. "This place has taught me to cook, which was my dream. Now, working with Attica, it seems like my dreams have come true," he says, echoing the sense that in terms of emotional well-being, this is perhaps one of the most generous staff meals of all.

Australian Tom Yum

← p. 44

1 Place the chicken stock in a large pan over a medium heat and bring to a gentle simmer. Season with salt and sugar to taste.

2 Place the lemongrass, shallots, cilantro (coriander) roots, chiles, galangal, and kaffir lime leaves in a large mortar and pestle and grind to a coarse paste. Add to the stock and simmer for 1.5 minutes.

3 Place individual serving bowls on the work counter (work surface).

4 Divide the mussels and noodles between serving bowls.

5 Cut the limes in half and squeeze the juice of one whole lime into each bowl. Divide the fish sauce between the bowls. Divide the cilantro (coriander) leaves between the bowls and then ladle in the soup. Serve immediately.

	for 2	for 6	for 20	for 50
light chicken stock	2 cups/500 ml	6 cups/1.4 L	22 cups/4.75 L	–
lemongrass stalks, cut into 2-inch (5-cm) sections	1	3	10	–
purple shallots, finely chopped	2	6	20	–
cilantro (coriander) roots	1	3	10	–
small green chiles	3	9	30	–
galangal, cut into ¼-inch (½-cm)-thick slices	1	3	10	–
kaffir lime leaves	4	12	40	–
steamed, shelled mussels	15	45	140	–
thin rice noodles, lightly cooked	4 oz/125 g	11 oz/375 g	2½ lb/1.2 kg	–
fresh limes	2	6	20	–
Thai fish sauce	4 tsp	4 tbsp	scant 1 cup/200 ml	–
cilantro (coriander) leaves	2 large pinches	6 large pinches	20 large pinches	–
sugar	to taste	to taste	to taste	–
salt	to taste	to taste	to taste	–

Butter Chicken

1 Combine the plain (natural) yogurt, lemon juice, turmeric, salt, garam masala and cumin and pour over the chicken, making sure that it is thoroughly coated.

2 Cover and place in the refrigerator for 24 hours to marinate.

3 In a large pan, melt the butter and oil over medium heat. Stir in the onions and cook for about 10 minutes until translucent. Stir in the garlic, ginger, and cumin seeds and cook for 3 minutes longer or until the onions are lightly browned.

4 Add the cinnamon sticks, diced tomatoes and chiles to the pan and season with salt, then cook over medium heat for 10 minutes.

5 Stir in the chicken and marinade and cook for another 5 minutes.

6 Add the chicken broth (stock) to the pan, bring to a boil, and then simmer for 30 minutes.

7 Stir in the cream and tomato paste (puree). Continue to cook for another 10–15 minutes or until the chicken is cooked through.

8 Stir in the almond meal (ground almonds) and cook for a final 5 minutes. Serve garnished with cilantro (coriander) leaves.

	for 2	for 6	for 20	for 50
plain (natural) yogurt	½ cup/120 ml	1½ cups/350 ml	4¼ cups/1 L	10½ cups/2.5 L
lemon juice	2 tsp	2 tbsp	6 tbsp	1 cup/250 ml
turmeric powder	1½ tsp	1½ tbsp	4 tbsp	10 tbsp
garam masala	1½ tsp	2 tbsp	6 tbsp	15 tbsp
ground cumin	1½ tsp	2 tbsp	6 tbsp	15 tbsp
chicken breasts or thighs, skinned	1 lb 2 oz/500 g	3 lb/1.4 kg	9 lb/4 kg	22 lb/10 kg
unsalted butter	3 tbsp	1 stick/¼ lb/135 g	3½ sticks/14 oz/400 g	8 sticks/2 lb/900 g
vegetable oil	1 tsp	4 tsp	4 tbsp	10 tbsp
onions, finely chopped	1 small	2	6	15
garlic, peeled and finely chopped	3 cloves	10 cloves	2 heads	5 heads
fresh ginger, peeled and grated	1 tbsp	3 tbsp	½ cup/120 g	1¼ cups/300 g
cumin seeds	1 tbsp	¼ cup/45 g	¾ cup/140 g	scant 2 cups/350 g
cinnamon sticks	½ small	1	4	10
canned diced tomatoes	3½ oz/100 g	7 oz/200 g	1 lb 5 oz/600 g	3¼ lb/1.5 kg
fresh red chiles, sliced	1	1 oz/30 g	3½ oz/100 g	9 oz/250 g
chicken broth (stock)	4 tbsp	⅔ cup/150 ml	1⅔ cups/400 ml	4¼ cups/1 L
heavy (double) cream	½ cup/120 ml	1½ cups/350 ml	4¼ cups/1 L	2½ qt/2.5 L
tomato paste (puree)	½ tsp	1½ tsp	4 tbsp	10 tbsp
almond meal (ground almonds)	1 tbsp	3 tbsp	⅔ cup/65 g	1⅔ cups/165 g
cilantro (fresh coriander) leaves, to garnish	3 sprigs	½ small bunch	small bunch	2 large bunches
salt, to taste				

Daal

1 Wash the lentils and cook in a saucepan of boiling water for 30 minutes or until tender.

2 Meanwhile, heat the mustard oil in a skillet or frying pan, add the cumin seeds, and fry for 1 minute until fragrant.

3 Add the ginger, onions, and garlic to the pan and cook, stirring occasionally, for about 10–15 minutes until the onions are golden brown.

4 Add the water to the pan followed by the tomatoes and chiles and bring to a simmer for 10–15 minutes.

5 Turn the heat to low and add the turmeric, garam masala, curry powder, dried fenugreek, salt and black pepper and cook for another 5–10 minutes.

6 Drain the lentils and then add to the skillet and stir to combine. Bring the mixture back to a simmer and continue to cook for 15 minutes. Serve warm, garnished with fresh cilantro (coriander).

	for 2	for 6	for 20	for 50
green lentils	⅔ cup/120 g	1¾ cups/350 g	5 cups/1 kg	12½ cups/2.5 kg
yellow lentils	⅓ cup/70 g	1 cup/200 g	3 cups/600 g	7½ cups/1.5 kg
mustard oil	2 tbsp	scant ½ cup/100 ml	1¼ cups/300 ml	3¾ cups/900 ml
cumin seeds	1 tbsp	⅓ cup/30 g	1 cup/100 g	2½ cups/250 g
fresh ginger, peeled and finely chopped	5 tsp	½ cup/40 g	1¼ cups/120 g	3 cups/300 g
onions, sliced	1 small	1 cup/120 g	3 cups/350 g	7½ cups/875 g
cloves garlic, finely chopped	3 cloves	10 cloves	2 heads/120 g	5 heads/300 g
water	5 tbsp	1 cup/250 ml	1¾ cups/400 ml	3 cups/750 ml
canned diced tomatoes	3 tbsp	½ cup/120 g	1½ cups/350 g	3¾ cups/875 g
fresh green chiles, chopped	1	3	10	25
turmeric powder	1½ tsp	1½ tbsp	4 tbsp	10 tbsp
garam masala	1½ tsp	1½ tbsp	4 tbsp	10 tbsp
curry powder	½ tsp	2 tsp	2 tbsp	5 tbsp
dried fenugreek leaves	1 tbsp	4 tbsp	¾ cup/45 g	2 cups/120 g
cilantro (coriander) leaves, to garnish	4 sprigs	½ small bunch	1 bunch	2 bunches
salt and black pepper, to taste				

Rice

1 Preheat the oven to 250°F/120°C/gas mark ½.

2 Rinse the rice thoroughly in cold water until the water runs clear. Put the rice in a saucepan or large roasting pan with the remaining ingredients.

3 Bring to a boil over high heat. Stir well and cover. Cook in the preheated oven for 15–20 minutes or until the water has been absorbed and the rice is just cooked.

4 Remove from the oven and set aside to rest, covered, for 5 minutes.

5 Uncover and fluff the rice gently with a fork. Serve immediately.

	for 2	for 6	for 20	for 50
basmati rice	¾ cup/120 g	2½ cups/450 g	8 cups/1.5 kg	19½ cups/8 lb/3.6 kg
cinnamon sticks, broken in half	½	1	2	5
cumin seeds	¼ tsp	½ tsp	1 tsp	1 tbsp
whole cloves	1	4	12	25
salt	¼ tsp	½ tsp	2 tsp	5 tsp
water	1½ cups/350 ml	4¼ cups/1 L	12¾ cups/3 L	8 qt/7.5 L

← A meat dish served in the empty dining room (previous page).

← Peter Gunn digs in to some tom yum.

↑ Daniel Elliot (front), Hannah Green (left), and Clinton Surrex (right), (top). The Attica family meal is served while work continues on the rotary evaporator behind.

↑ Pascale Beirouti (above).

→ Sharing a meal are Banjo Harris-Plane, Clinton Surrex, and Nikolaos Pouloupatis (overleaf).

Blue Hill at Stone Barns

Location
Pocantico Hills, New York, USA

Established
2004

Head chef
Dan Barber

← Weekly staff meeting in the garden (previous pages).

← The custom-made barbecue is put to good use to cook simple yet delicious staff food, such as this grilled flank steak.

↑ Adam Kaye (left) and Michael Gallina (right). The barbecue was custom-made for Blue Hill at Stone Barns by Grillworks. It weighs nearly 1 ton (900 kg), is more than 9 feet (2.7 meters) long, and is one of the restaurant's most versatile tools, used for everything from slow-roasting to steaming.

→ Michael Gallina, chef de cuisine (overleaf).

Blue Hill at Stone Barns

Blue Hill goes way beyond the remit of most restaurants: it's more of a "university of food." Situated on an estate owned by the Rockefellers, it covers a huge open area of lakes and woodland, hills and plains, and an organic farm fully stocked with pigs, chickens, geese, and other animals as well as greenhouses and gardens. The restaurant is its heart and soul, and almost 100-percent self-sufficient.

Such a huge operation requires a massive team, and once a week everyone meets up to share in what is fondly known as "Thursday's all-farm family meal." It's a rare opportunity to bring together the people who make it happen, not just those in the restaurant but also farmers, gardeners, and teachers at the education center. It allows them to interact, tell stories, exchange ideas, and learn about what's going on within their industry. "We're sort of like a marriage," says Stone Barns Center's head vegetable farmer, Jack Algiere. "We need to do one of those date nights every week just so we can actually talk."

Often they invite guest speakers, too: slow-food farmers, mushroom foragers, plant breeders, winemakers, or soil scientists, who present their work and answer questions before sitting down to a meal with everyone else. And because the farm is a nonprofit organization, some three thousand school-children pass through each year to learn about farming, growing, preparing, and cooking real food. This is what really sets Blue Hill apart from other ambitious Michelin restaurants: a mission not just to cook fantastic food, but to educate themselves, the wider community, and future generations about how things could be done. Blue Hill people have a thirst for knowledge about anything related to food, and that's a big part of the culture.

The family meal is also an extension of a belief system that is deeply connected to the land and grounded in old-fashioned, waste-not-want-not cooking. There are no menus for either the dining room or the family meal. Dishes are planned by seasons, which could be as brief as a couple of weeks, combined with the weekly butchering of various home-reared, happy animals.

If the weather allows, these meals take the form of a big barbecue: grilled meat and corn, homemade pasta with sauce made from scraps, and huge pans of the most beautiful focaccia you've ever seen topped with luscious tomatoes, bright and glossy and plucked from the garden minutes earlier. Afterward, people sip infusions made from herbs gathered in the garden and discuss the day's new insights and how they might shape the future.

Using the staff meal as a serious platform for a community-driven, holistic education is an inspired concept, adding a whole new dimension to the restaurant business as we know it.

Emmer Wheat Foccacia

→ p. 68

1   First make the tomato powder. Place the tomato skins in a dehydrator and process according to the manufacturer's directions. Alternatively, place the skins in a single layer on paper towels (kitchen paper) and cover with another layer of towels. Microwave until dry and crisp. Let cool.

2   Grind the skins to a powder in a spice grinder. Keep in an airtight jar until required.

3   For the dough, put the water, yeast, and sugar into the large bowl of a stand mixer. Let stand for 5 minutes.

4   Add the flours, olive oil, salt, and tomato powder. Mix on low speed until a cohesive dough is formed, adding more all-purpose (plain) flour, if required.

5   Cover the dough with oiled plastic wrap (clingfilm) and refrigerate for at least 4 hours or overnight.

6   Meanwhile, make the tomato sauce. Put the olive oil in a saucepan over medium-low heat. Stir in the onions. Cook until softened, then add the garlic. Cook for another minute. Add the plum tomatoes. Season with salt and black pepper.

7   Cook until the tomatoes are softened and the excess liquid has cooked away. Adjust seasoning and let cool.

8   Oil a lipped baking sheet large enough to contain the dough to a thickness of 1 inch (2.5 cm). Stretch the dough to fill the pan. Cover with oiled plastic wrap (clingfilm) and let stand at room temperature for 1–1½ hours or until the dough has doubled in size.

9   Preheat the oven to 425°F/225°C/gas mark 7. Spread the top of the dough with the tomato sauce and top with the heirloom tomato slices. Sprinkle with sea salt.

10 Bake in the middle of the oven for 20–25 minutes until cooked through and beginning to brown. Cool on a wire rack for 20 minutes before serving.

for the tomato powder	for 2	for 6	for 20	for 50
tomato skins	–	¾ oz/20 g	2 oz/50 g	4 oz/120 g

for the dough	for 2	for 6	for 20	for 50
warm water	–	½ cup/120 ml	1¾ cups/400 ml	3½ cups/800 ml
active dry (fast action) yeast	–	1 tsp	1½ packets/11 g	2¼ tbsp
granulated sugar	–	½ tsp	1 tsp	2 tsp
emmer wheat (farro), finely ground	–	⅔ cup/140 g	9 oz/250 g	2¾ cups/500 g
all-purpose (plain) flour	–	1½ tbsp	1½ oz/40 g	¾ cup/3½ oz
olive oil	–	1 tbsp	4 tbsp	scant ½ cup/100 ml
salt	–	2 tsp	1 tbsp	2 tbsp
heirloom tomatoes, sliced ¼-inch (5-mm) thick	–	1	3	5
sea salt, for sprinkling	–	to taste	to taste	to taste

for the tomato sauce	for 2	for 6	for 20	for 50
olive oil	–	1 tbsp	2 tbsp	5 tbsp
onion, finely chopped	–	4 tbsp	¾ cup/100 g	1½ cups/250 g
garlic cloves, crushed	–	1	2	4
plum tomatoes, seeded and diced	–	3	10	20
salt and black pepper	–	to taste	to taste	to taste

Pork Parts Bolognese

→ p. 65

1 Grind the pork trimmings, organ meats (offal), and salumi scraps through the coarse plate of a meat grinder or chop coarsely in a food processor.

2 Heat the oil in a Dutch oven or casserole dish and brown the ground meat, pig foot (trotter), and bones. Season with salt and black pepper. With a slotted spoon, transfer the meat to a bowl and set aside.

3 Preheat the oven to 350°F/180°C/gas mark 4.

4 Heat the oil over medium heat, add the onion, carrots, celery, and fennel and cook until golden. Stir in the garlic and cook for another 30 seconds.

5 Return the meat to the pot, then add the oregano and red pepper (chili) flakes. Stir to combine, then cook for 2 minutes.

6 Add the red wine and reduce by three-quarters. Add the tomatoes, bay leaves, rosemary, and Parmesan rind. Bring to a simmer on top of the stove, then place in the oven and cook for 3 hours, or until the pig foot (trotter) is soft and begins to fall apart.

7 Remove the pot from the oven and return to the stove top. Carefully remove the pig foot (trotter) and bones. Set aside and let cool.

8 When cool enough to handle, pick off as much meat and skin as possible. Chop the meat coarsely and return to the pot. Discard the bones, bay leaves, rosemary sprig, and Parmesan rind. Stir in the basil chiffonade. Season to taste and serve with pasta and grated Parmesan cheese.

	for 2	for 6	for 20	for 50
pork trimmings	–	12 oz/350 g	4 lb/1.8 kg	8¾ lb/4 kg
pork organ meats (offal), such as liver, heart, kidney	–	6 oz/175 g	1¼ lb/575 g	2¾ lb/1.3 kg
salumi scraps	–	1 oz/30 g	4 oz/120 g	10 oz/275 kg
pig foot (trotter)	–	1	1	2
meaty pork rib bones	–	1	4	8
olive oil	–	1 tbsp	4 tbsp	10 tbsp
onions, finely chopped	–	½	2 large	4 large
carrots, finely chopped	–	½	2 large	4 large
celery stalk, finely chopped	–	½	2	3
fennel, finely chopped	–	¼ head	1 head	2 heads
garlic cloves, crushed	–	2	6	12
dried oregano	–	1 tsp	1 tbsp	2 tbsp
red pepper (chili) flakes	–	½ tsp	1 tsp	2 tsp
red wine	–	4 tbsp	1½ cups/350 ml	3 cups/750 ml
canned crushed tomatoes	–	2 cups/475 g	12 cups/3 kg	14 lb/6.3 kg
bay leaves	–	½	2	4
sprig of rosemary	–	½	1	2
piece of Parmesan rind	–	1 inch/2.5 cm	5 inches/12 cm	10 inches/25 cm
basil leaves, finely sliced	–	1 sprig	6 sprigs	12 sprigs
salt and black pepper	–	to taste	to taste	to taste

Quark Pillows with Wapsie Valley Corn and Grilled Peaches

→ p. 67

1 First make the dough. Using the hook attachment of a stand mixer, combine the dry ingredients. Add the butter and quark and mix until just combined.

2 Form the dough into a ball, cover with plastic wrap (clingfilm), and refrigerate overnight.

3 Remove the dough from the plastic wrap and divide into 4 equal pieces. Roll each piece into a ¼-inch (5-mm)-thick sheet and stamp out 3.5-inch (9-cm) circles, using a cookie cutter. Place the circles on a baking sheet lined with parchment paper, cover, and refrigerate for 1 hour.

4 Meanwhile, prepare the peaches. Place the peach halves flesh side down on the grill (barbecue) for 4–5 minutes over medium-high heat. Remove the peaches from the grill and transfer to a baking sheet. Cover with a towel or plastic wrap for 2–3 minutes, then remove the skin.

5 Preheat the oven to 400°F/200°C/gas mark 6.

6 Place ½ of a grilled peach in the center of each circle of dough and shape the dough into a triangle. Brush each "pillow" with egg wash and sprinkle lightly with confectioners' (icing) sugar.

7 Transfer to the oven and bake 10–15 minutes until golden.

8 Transfer the pillows to a wire rack to cool.

	for 2	for 6	for 20	for 50
all-purpose (plain) flour	⅔ cup/75 g	1¾ cups/225 g	6 cups/750 g	–
dried Wapsie Valley corn, freshly ground	2 tbsp	½ cup/65 g	1½ cups/200 g	–
salt	pinch	½ tsp	1 tsp	–
butter	6 tbsp	2 sticks/½ lb/225 g	7 sticks/1¾ lb/825 g	–
quark cheese	5 tbsp	1 cup/225 g	3¾ cups/825 g	–
very ripe peaches, halved and pits removed	1	3	10	–
eggs, beaten	1	1	2	–
confectioners' (icing) sugar	1 tbsp	2 tbsp	4 tbsp	–

← Pork Parts Bolognese (p. 63), (previous page).

← The Emmer Wheat Foccacia (p. 62).

↑ Quark Pillows with Wapsie Valley Corn and Grilled Peaches (p. 64).

→ The Emmer Wheat Foccacia (p. 62) is served up (overleaf).

Blue Hill at Stone Barns

Il Canto

Location
Siena, Italy

Established
2002

Head chef
Paolo Lopriore

← (previous page) Gianluca Gorini: foraging for herbs in the monastery gardens provides a peaceful moment.

↑ Gianluca Gorini at work in the kitchen.

→ Staff dining room with a view.
→ Capocollo (p. 80, overleaf).

Il Canto

Chef Paolo Lopriore is a culinary artist who uses ingredients as a painter might use fine oils or watercolor pigments. His backdrop is the Certosa de Maggiano, a Carthusian monastery built in 1314 whose church still celebrates Mass on Sundays; and his medium is the produce of the surrounding farms and gardens from which the restaurant takes its name. Like most artists he walks an independent path, being less concerned with Michelin stars than with creating dishes that have integrity and are a true expression of his beloved country.

While many chefs today are zooming into the future with modernist techniques and show-stopping theater, Lopriore has returned to the traditional in terms of the food, the dining experience, and the inherent values of Il Canto. His flavors are honest and unpretentious, his staff an extension of family.

Il Canto is all about relationships: with the produce, with the land, and with each other. It consists of a small team of just four or five, with Lopriore nurturing each of them much like a father. He guides them through the monastery's quite wild-seeming gardens, little changed from when the monks were still cultivating the land, and shows them how to translate that natural abundance onto the plate. Their closeness to each other and to local suppliers mean that friendships form quickly, and within that framework the staff meal has become an almost sacred ritual that Paolo insists on cooking himself even though he rarely joins them. "You've got to show your people you care," he says, "but it's also essential that they have some space and privacy to be themselves."

For the team, it is an intimate time, with the bonus of being treated to Paolo at his most spontaneous. The meal is built on whatever he has been offered by local farmers, plucked from their own gardens or foraged from the shrubs. "I want them to immerse themselves heart and stomach in their immediate environment," he says of his staff, "and to form their own ideas about what this food should be."

His generosity of spirit combined with unexpected freedom is what makes working here so rewarding. It allows the team to flourish beyond conventional borders. Most important of all is the learning to be gained from Lopriore's own example: care not about what others think, but more about what matters to you.

Saffron Risotto

→ p. 81

1   Heat most of the butter in a skillet or frying pan and sauté the onions, stirring constantly, for 2 minutes until translucent.

2   Add the rice to the pan and let it toast in the butter for a short time.

3   Add the wine to the pan and cook for 3 minutes until the alcohol has evaporated.

4   Add 2 ladlefuls of chicken broth (stock) and continue stirring until the liquid is absorbed.

5   Continue to add ladlefuls of broth, stirring constantly, as the rice absorbs the liquid.

6   The rice is cooked when it is soft on the outside but still retains a slight bite in the middle.

7   Add the saffron, Parmesan cheese, and remaining butter to the risotto and continue to stir for a few minutes more.

8   Serve warm.

	for 2	for 6	for 20	for 50
butter	2 tbsp	6 tbsp	1½ sticks/6 oz/175 g	–
onion, finely chopped	½ small	1 medium	2 large	–
risotto rice	1 cup/175 g	2¾ cups/500 g	8 cups/1.5 kg	–
dry white wine	4 tbsp	¾ cup/175 ml	2⅓ cups/550 ml	–
chicken or vegetable broth (stock)	1 cup/250 ml	3 cups/700 ml	8½ cups/2 L	–
good quality saffron stamens	pinch	1 tsp	1 tbsp	–
Parmesan cheese, grated	1 cup/75 g	2 cups/175 g	6 cups/500 g	–

Bresaola and Finocchielle

1   Clean and finely slice the bresaola and finocchielle.
Set aside.

2   Combine the olive oil and lemon juice to make a vinaigrette,
season to taste, and beat well to combine.

3   Arrange the sliced finocchielle on a serving plate and pour
over half of the vinaigrette.

4   Top with the sliced bresaola and pour over the remaining
vinaigrette.

5   Serve immediately.

	for 2	for 6	for 20	for 50
bresaola (sliced air-dried salted beef)	2 oz/60 g	7 oz/200 g	1 lb 5 oz/600 g	3¼ lb/1.5 kg
finocchiele (cured Italian salami)	2 oz/60 g	7 oz/200 g	1 lb 5 oz/600 g	3¼ lb/1.5 kg

for the vinaigrette				
extra virgin olive oil	3 tbsp	6 tbsp	¾ cup/175 ml	2 cups/500 ml
lemon, juiced	½	1	3	7
salt and black pepper	to taste	to taste	to taste	to taste

Capocollo Pork

1. Trim most of the surface fat from the pork using a sharp knife. Make ¼-inch (5-mm) incisions over the surface of the meat.

2. With a mortar and pestle, or in a food processor, crush the juniper berries, black peppercorns, and garlic. Use to fill the incisions in the pork. Tie the meat at intervals with string to keep its shape.

3. Heat half of the olive oil in a skillet or frying pan and brown the meat on all sides over high heat. If making larger quantities, the pork will need to be cut into a size to fit the skillet. Set the meat aside.

4. Put the remaining olive oil in the pan over low heat. Add the onions. Cook, stirring frequently, until the onions are soft and translucent.

5. Transfer the meat and the onions to a large, deep saucepan and add the vinegar and the wine. Season with salt and black pepper then add enough water to cover the meat.

6. Bring to the simmer, cover, and cook for 90 minutes.

7. Remove the meat from the pan, and remove and discard the string. Slice the pork and season to taste. Serve on a bed of onions.

	for 2	for 6	for 20	for 50
pork shoulder	–	1½ lb/700 g	4½ lb/2 kg	11 lb/5 kg
juniper berries	–	6	18	45
bay leaves	–	5	15	37
black peppercorns	–	2 tsp	1 tbsp	2 tbsp
cloves garlic, crushed	–	1	4	10
extra virgin olive oil	–	4 tbsp	¾ cup/175 ml	2 cups/500 ml
red onions, sliced	–	5	6¾ lb/3 kg	16½ lb/7.5 kg
white vinegar	–	1 cup/250 ml	3 cups/700 ml	7½ cups/1.8 L
white wine	–	4 tbsp	¾ cup/175 ml	2 cups/500 ml
salt and black pepper	–	to taste	to taste	to taste

← Saffron Risotto (p. 78, previous page).
← Sommelier Michele Baldantoni enjoys an apricot.

↑ The Strada di Certosa is an integral part of restaurant life, running right through the old monastery and church.

→ Il Canto's staff meal has become an almost sacred ritual. From left to right: Robin di Dio, Giovanni Astolfoni, and Michele Baldantoni (overleaf).

El Celler de Can Roca

Location
Girona, Spain

Established
1986

Head chef
Joan Roca

← Every day the entire team walk a couple of minutes up the hill from the famous restaurant to eat lunch at the Roca brothers' parent's village bistro, Can Roca (previous page).

← "For me, staff meal is just like feeding one big, happy, extended family." Montserrat Fontané, the Roca brothers' mother.

↑ Montserrat's legendary *calamares à la romana* (Squid Rings in Batter, p. 94).

→ Jordi Roca: *botifarra amb mongetes* (sausage and beans), is the most emblematic of Catalan country dishes (overleaf).

El Celler de Can Roca

El Celler de Can Roca

I'd heard stories about the family meal at El Celler de Can Roca long before I ever ate there. Every day, the story went, the Roca brothers—Joan, Jordi, and Josep—along with their entire staff would walk a couple of minutes up the hill from their restaurant to eat lunch at their parents' village bistro, also called Can Roca. This ritual intrigued me. It wasn't just about going to get fed, it was about going home and, in that sense, perhaps the most "family" meal of them all.

El Celler de Can Roca is a big-scale operation staffed by a young team who come from all over the world, which can feel quite isolating. Going home to "mother" daily gives them a sense of belonging. When I eventually experienced a family meal with the team, Joan, the eldest of the three brothers, explained: "We grew up at Can Roca. The dining room was our playroom. It was very simple, very popular, and all about connecting with the people in our community. It still is, but it is also important to us that our team makes the physical journey to reconnect with the traditional cooking of the region, to get to know the products and centralize themselves in Catalunya in order to understand what we do and who we are at El Celler."

The brothers aren't alone in wanting to maintain a close connection to their roots. Montserrat, the brothers' mother, also stands by the importance of breaking bread together. "Now my boys are grown-up and celebrities, it's more important than ever to get this special moment every day to be together, and to remember where we come from," she says. "Cooking for personnel is a pleasure. It's what I've done all my life. It's just like feeding one big, happy, extended family, and I love that when they leave, they nearly all come back to visit."

As you might expect, the staff meal at Can Roca contains some serious Catalan home cooking. Montserrat is in charge and cooks hearty no-nonsense dishes from the region. As the brothers gather around the stainless steel workbenches of the compact kitchen chatting with their parents, the team bustle to and from the dining room helping themselves from a couple of huge pots of stewed lentils or grilled *botifarra* (pork sausages), plates of seasonal vegetables or salads, and, always, Montserrat's legendary *calamares à la romana* (squid rings in batter).

During the short staff meal the pressure is off for half an hour, and the atmosphere is friendly, warm, and noisy. As friends from the neighborhood stream through the door for lunch, I'm reminded why everything they do at Can Roca is so very important. Coming as I do from the north of Sweden, where I sometimes feel we've forgotten the value of coming together over food, I regard the nurturing nature of this staff meal, deeply rooted in the philosophy of both restaurants, as an example to us all.

Squid Rings in Batter

← p. 91

1   Clean the squid tubes and remove the outer membrane. Separate the tentacles from the innards. Discard the innards and outer membrane.

2   Slice the squid tubes into ½-inch (1-cm) rings.

3   To make the batter, combine the flour, water, Cognac, salt, eggs, and baking soda (bicarbonate of soda) in a large bowl and whisk until smooth.

4   Heat the oil in a large saucepan or deep fryer to 340°F/175°C.

5   Place some flour in a bowl and pass the squid rings and tentacles through the flour to coat.

6   Working in batches, pass the squid through the batter and then directly into the hot oil. Cook for around 1 minute until crisp and golden.

7   Remove the squid from the oil using a slotted spoon and drain on kitchen paper towels. Serve hot.

	for 2	for 6	for 20	for 50
large squid tubes	8 oz/225 g	1 lb 5 oz/600 g	4½ lb/2 kg	–
all-purpose (plain) flour	⅔ cup/75 g	1⅔ cups/200 g	4 cups/600 g	–
cold water	6 tbsp	1¼ cups/300 ml	3⅓ cups/800 ml	–
Cognac	2 tsp	4 tsp	4 tbsp	–
eggs, beaten	1 large	2 medium	4 large	–
baking soda (bicarbonate of soda)	¼ tsp	¾ tsp	2 tsp	–
mild-flavored olive oil	6⅓ cups/1.5 L	8½ cups/2 L	20 cups/5 L	–
salt	to taste	to taste	to taste	–

Holiday Cannelloni

1 Heat the oil in a frying pan over medium heat and add the beef, pork and chicken to brown. Add the garlic and grated onion to the meat. Reduce the heat to low, cover, and cook until the meat is tender.

2 Add the wine and brandy then cook, uncovered, stirring, until the liquid is reduced by half.

3 Add the liver and the lamb's brains and cook for a few minutes then stir in the grated tomato.

4 Soak the breadcrumbs in the first quantity of milk for a few minutes then drain in a sieve. Add the breadcrumbs to the meat. Allow the meat to cool to tepid then pass through a meat grinder. Season to taste.

5 Boil the lasagne sheets in salted water until pliable then submerge in cold water to stop the cooking. Place on a clean dish cloth in a single layer. Divide the meat mixture between the lasagne sheets and roll up to form cannelloni.

6 To prepare the Béchamel sauce, pour the milk into a pan and bring to the boil. In a second pan melt the butter. Remove from the heat and stir in the flour. Return to the heat and cook, stirring constantly, for a few minutes.

7 Slowly whisk in the hot milk, stirring constantly to ensure no lumps form. Bring to the boil and simmer for 2 minutes. Season to taste.

8 Heat the oven to 400°F/200°C/gas mark 6.

9 Spread a thin layer of Béchamel sauce over the base of a large lasagne dish. Place the cannelloni on top in a single layer then pour over the remaining sauce. Sprinkle over the Parmesan cheese.

10 Place in the oven for 30 minutes to heat through then preheat the broiler (grill) to high and brown the cannelloni. Serve immediately.

	for 2	for 6	for 20	for 50
olive oil		1 tbsp	3 tbsp	½ cup/120 ml
lean stewing beef, cubed		5 oz/150 g	1 lb/450 g	2½ lb/1.2 kg
lean pork loin or shoulder, cubed		5 oz/150 g	1 lb/450 g	2½ lb/1.2 kg
boneless, skinless chicken breast, cubed		3½ oz/100 g	10 oz/300 g	1 lb 10 oz/750 g
onion, grated		1 medium	3	5/1¼ lb/575 g
cloves garlic, sliced		2	7	1½ heads
white wine		3 tbsp	10 tbsp	1½ cups/350 ml
brandy		2 tbsp	3½ fl oz/100 ml	1 cup/250 ml
chicken liver, cleaned and coarsely chopped		1	3	8
lamb brains, cleaned and coarsely chopped		2 oz/60 g	6 oz/175 g	1 lb/450 g
large ripe tomato, grated		1	3	8
bread crumbs		2 slices of bread	6 slices of bread	18 slices of bread
milk		4 tbsp	¾ cup/175 ml	2 cups/500 ml
lasagna noodles (sheets)		12	40	100
salt		to taste	to taste	to taste

For the Béchamel sauce

	for 2	for 6	for 20	for 50
milk		4¼ cups/1 L	12 cups/3 L	7½ qt/7 L
butter		2 tbsp	6 tbsp	2 sticks/½ lb/225 g
all-purpose (plain) flour		2 tbsp	6 tbsp	1¾ cups/225 g
Parmesan cheese, grated		1⅓ cups/120 g	4 cups/340 g	1¾ lb/800 g
white pepper and freshly grated nutmeg		to taste	to taste	to taste

Rice Casserole

→ p. 97

1   Heat the olive oil in a large clay- or cast-iron pot over medium heat. Add the shrimp (prawns) and fry until firm and golden. Remove from the pan and set aside.

2   In the same pan brown the diced chicken, rabbit, and pork, adding more oil if necessary. Stir in the diced cuttlefish (or squid) and fry for an additional 3 minutes. Remove from the heat and set aside until needed.

3   Cook the onion and peppers in a separate pan for 10 minutes then add half the garlic and cook for a further 2 minutes, then add the onion, peppers, garlic, and wine (or brandy) to the meat.

4   After the alcohol has cooked off, add the grated tomatoes, rice, and peas. Pour over the boiling water.

5   Season to taste, bring to a gentle simmer, and cook, stirring occasionally for 15 minutes, until the rice is almost cooked but still has a slight bite.

6   Stir in the chicken liver, remaining garlic, cooked shrimp (prawns), parsley leaves, and cook for a further 2 minutes.

7   Remove from the heat and serve.

	for 2	for 6	for 20	for 50
olive oil	1 tbsp	2 tbsp	4 tbsp	½ cup/120 ml
large, raw, peeled shrimp (tiger prawns)	2	6	20	50
boneless, skinless chicken, cubed	2¾ oz/70 g	7 oz/200 g	1½ lb/675 g	3¾ lb/1.7 kg
boneless, skinless rabbit meat, cubed	2¾ oz/70 g	7 oz/200 g	1½ lb/675 g	3¾ lb/1.7 kg
boneless pork loin, cubed	2¾ oz/70 g	7 oz/200 g	1½ lb/675 g	3¾ lb/1.7 kg
cuttlefish or squid, cleaned and diced	1 small	1	4	10
onions, chopped	⅔ cup/100 g	1½ cups/225 g	4¼ cups/675 g	10½ cups/1.7 kg
green and red bell pepper, diced	2 tbsp	⅓ cup/50 g	⅔ cup/150 g	2½ cups/375 g
cloves garlic, chopped	1–2	5	15	38
fortified wine or brandy	2 tbsp	5 tbsp	1 cup/250 ml	2½ cups/600 ml
tomatoes, skinned and grated	1 small	2	6	15
Spanish rice or risotto	⅔ cup/120 g	2 cups/350 g	5¼ cups/1 kg	13 cups/2.5 kg
peas	⅓ cup/50 g	1 cup/150 g	3 cups/450 g	7½ cups/1.1 kg
water for boiling	2 cups/500 ml	6¼ cups/1.5 L	19 cups/4.5 L	12 qt/11.25 L
chicken liver, cleaned and diced	1 small	1	3	8
fresh parsley leaves	1 tbsp	2 tbsp	6 tbsp	1 cup/75 g
salt	to taste	to taste	to taste	to taste

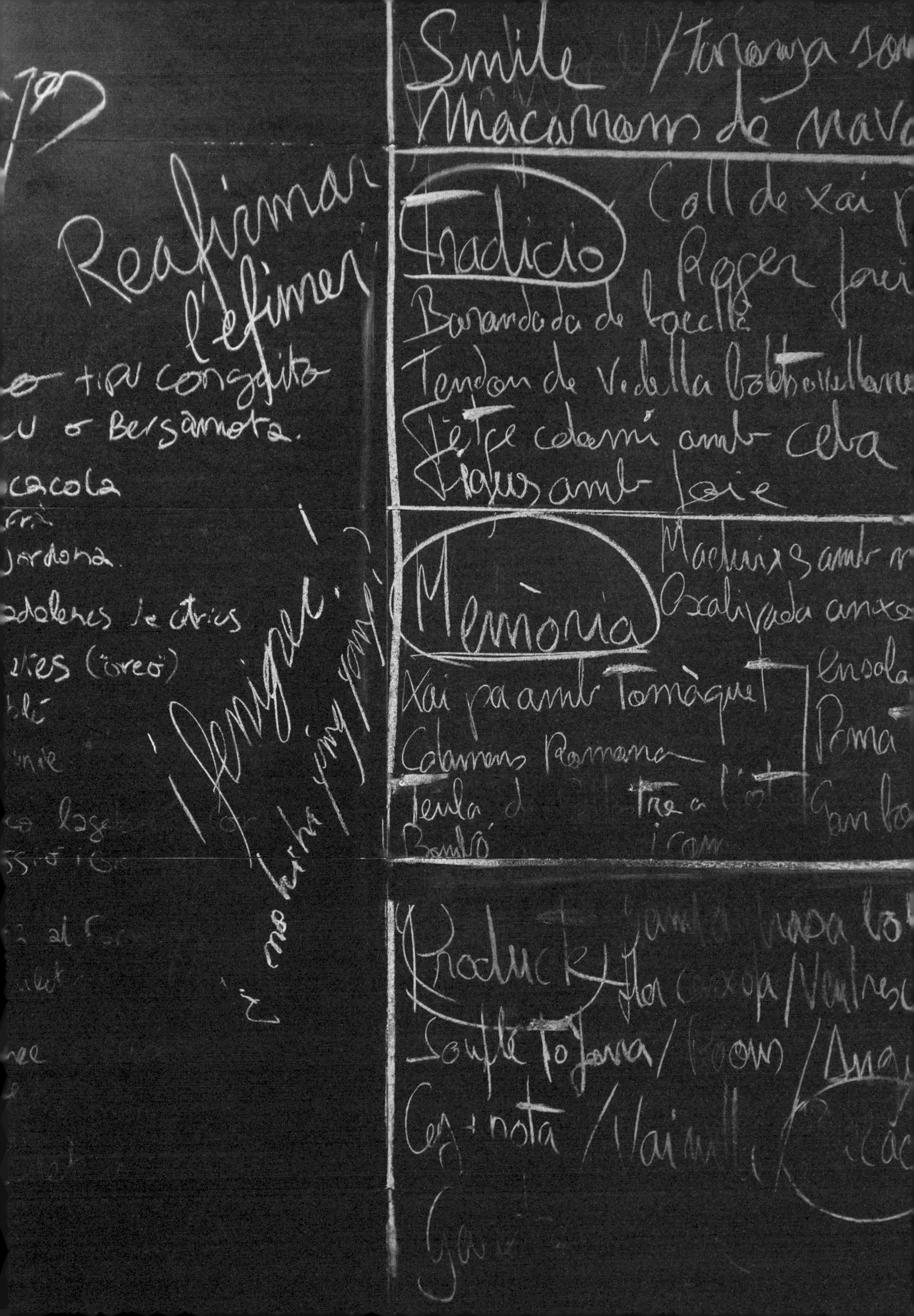

Reafirmar
l'efímer

...tipu congeits
...u o Bergamota.
...cacola
...fri
...ordona
...adolenes le otries
...ies (oreo)
...li
...nile
...lage
...ss...ies
...al r...
...let
...ree

¡Peníguel!

Smile /...
Macarrons de Nava...

Tradició
Borombada de paella
Tendon de v. della bóteravellan...
Pètge colemi amb ceba
Figues amb foie

Memòria
Xai pa amb Tomàquet
Calemars Romana
Teula d...
Bombó

Mòlluixs amb...
Escalivada amix...
Ensala...
Poma
Gamb...

Product
Soufle To Java / ...
Ceg + nota / Ai...

Coll de xai
Roger foui

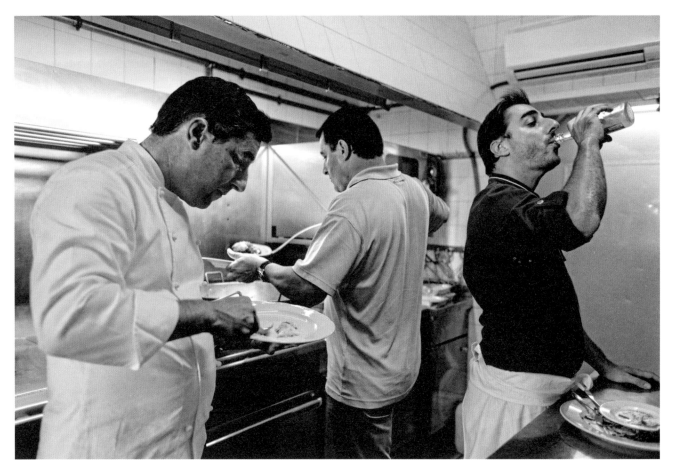

← Rice Casserole (p. 97, previous page).

← The holy trinity that all Can Roca dishes are built on: tradition, memory, product.

↑ From left to right: Joan, Josep, and Jordi. It's not just getting fed, it's going home.

→ Montserrat's dining room at the other Can Roca (overleaf).

The French Laundry

Location
Yountville, California, USA

Established
1994

Head chef
Thomas Keller

← In a patriotic gesture, the American flag is raised every morning at dawn (previous page).

↑ Timothy Hollingsworth takes the lead at the lunchtime staff buffet.

→ Aaron Keefer, second gardener and his "prison tray."

↑ Carolina BBQ Pork (p. 110).

The French Laundry

The name Thomas Keller packs a lot of weight in the United States. It refers not only to the famous chef and his style of fine dining, but also to a trend-setting kitchen that is hugely aspirational not only for those who eat there but also for the people that work there.

His restaurant is all about redefining American cooking. As a cuisine it has many different regional influences, which, you could argue, begin with the food eaten during the staff meal. People come to work here from all over the country (and, of course, from the rest of the world, too), and most of the staff meal cooking is grounded in doing American regional specialities really well, like proper Southern-style pulled pork or classic apple pie.

The French Laundry staff offers probably the best example in the world of the dishes that built modern American cuisine, and points to the future of casual dining. Comfort food like pulled-pork buns, elegant barbecue, and fancy fried chicken has been embraced as restaurant themes from Louisiana to London. Much of it has been perfected in restaurant staff meals all over America, but no one does it with quite the finesse of the team behind Keller.

Every second is precious. People eat fast and rush back to their stations, but you never lose the sense that it's the food and the cooking that are important. This is a place of perfectionists. They have this incredible eye for detail, from the rigor and skill with which everything is prepared to an almost obsessive level of patriotism—the American flag is raised every morning at dawn—and precision.

Order is everything. Staff refer good-humoredly to their cafeteria-style, compartmentalized trays as "prison plates," which look hilarious because it's the antithesis of the fine-dining mold: fruit, soup, vegetables, meat, and dessert all together. And structurally it's like an extension of service, because dining room staff are responsible not only for making up their own plate but also for making up a plate for one of the kitchen staff. "We've always put a strong emphasis on doing a great staff meal in the right way," says sous chef Michael Wallace. "I think it's pretty amazing that we can cook as great as we do for staff when everybody's so busy, but that's because we've organized the staff meal the same way we organize everything else."

The French Laundry staff meal, then, is like a mirror image of the restaurant. Whether meatball sandwiches or rice pudding, eaten standing up at the stove or outside on the lawn as if it were a big sophisticated picnic, it is always a celebration of American regional food done with incredible care, skill, and attention to detail.

Carolina BBQ Pork

→ p. 108

Start this recipe at least 4 days before you plan to serve it.

1 Place half the water, the salts, and sugar in a deep saucepan. Bring to a boil to dissolve the salts and sugar. Add the remaining ingredients and water for the brine. Cool to room temperature, then add the pork. Cover and refrigerate for 2–3 days.

2 For the spice rub, place the fennel seeds, peppercorns, cloves, and cumin seeds in a dry skillet or frying pan over low heat. Cook, stirring, for 2 minutes until fragrant. Add the remaining spices and cook, stirring for another 30 seconds. Turn onto a plate to cool, then grind in a spice grinder or mortar and pestle.

3 Remove the pork from the brine and pat dry. Sprinkle the spice mixture on a large piece of waxed (greaseproof) paper. Place the pork on top of the spices and rub them into the pork. Place the pork on a wire rack over a roasting pan. Cover loosely with foil and refrigerate for 24 hours.

4 Soak apple wood chips in water for 15 minutes. Preheat the oven to 250°F/125°C/gas mark 1. Drain the wood chips in a colander. Place one-quarter of the wood chips in a roasting pan in the bottom third of the oven. Place the pork on the rack over the second roasting pan in the middle of the oven. Smoke for 2 hours, adding an additional quarter of the wood chips every half hour.

5 To braise the pork place all of the ingredients in a Dutch oven (casserole dish) then nestle the pork in the vegetables. Turn the oven temperature up to 325°F/160°C/gas mark 3. Cover and cook for 3 hours, until the pork is tender.

6 While the pork is still warm pull into shreds. Serve the shredded pork with the barbecue sauce.

	for 2	for 6	for 20	for 50
Boston butt or pork shoulder roast	–	3¼ lb/1.5 kg	10 lb/4.5 kg	25 lb/10 kg
for the brine				
water	–	8½ cups/2 L	24 cups/5.7 L	12 qt/11.4 L
kosher salt	–	⅓ cup/100 g	1⅓ cups/300 g	3⅓ cups/750 g
pink sea salt	–	3 tbsp	¾ cup/150 g	1¾ cups/350 g
granulated sugar	–	4 tbsp	¾ cup/150 g	2 cups/400 g
garlic cloves, bruised	–	1	3	6
fresh thyme sprigs	–	3	10	20
juniper berries	–	3	10	25
strips of orange zest	–	2	6	10
for the spice rub				
fennel seeds	–	1½ tbsp	4 tbsp	1 cup/100 g
black peppercorns	–	½ tsp	2 tsp	2 tbsp
cloves	–	5	15	30
cumin seeds	–	2 tsp	2 tbsp	½ cup/50 g
English mustard powder	–	4 tsp	1½ tbsp	3½ tbsp
ground allspice	–	2 tsp	2 tbsp	5 tbsp
ground cinnamon	–	1 tsp	1 tbsp	2 tbsp
smoked paprika	–	5 tbsp	1 cup/120 g	2 cups/250 g
for the braise				
yellow onions, diced	–	2	3	6
fennel, diced	–	1 medium	3 medium	10
large carrots	–	2 tbsp	handful	1 large bunch
heads of garlic	–	½	1½	4
fresh thyme sprigs	–	1 oz/25 g	1 oz/25 g	2½ oz/65 g
chicken stock	–	2 cups/500 ml	6 cups/1.5 L	15 cups/3.5 L

Carolina BBQ Sauce

→ p. 108

1   Put the oil in a nonreactive saucepan that will hold the quantity of sauce you are making, then add the onions. Cook over low heat until softened.

2   Add the remaining ingredients in the order listed. Bring to a low simmer and cook for 30 minutes, stirring occasionally. The mixture will thicken when cool.

3   Let cool then store in glass jars in the refrigerator.

	for 2	for 6	for 20	for 50
canola (rapeseed) oil	–	1 tbsp	3 tbsp	5 tbsp
onions, finely chopped	–	½ medium	2 medium	4 medium
English mustard powder	–	1½ tsp	1½ tbsp	4 tbsp
ground celery seed	–	pinch	½ tsp	1¼ tsp
ground cayenne, to taste	–	½–1 tsp	½–1 tbsp	1½–2½ tbsp
ground Spanish paprika	–	1½ tsp	1½ tbsp	3½ tbsp
allspice	–	½ tsp	½ tbsp	1½ tbsp
tomato ketchup	–	2 cups/500 ml	6½ cups/1.5 L	12½ cups/3 L
Worcestershire sauce	–	½ tsp	2 tsp	5 tsp
white vinegar	–	1 cup/250 ml	3 cups/700 ml	6½ cups/1.5 L
cider vinegar	–	1 cup/250 ml	3 cups/700 ml	6½ cups/1.5 L

Apple Compote with Apple Streusel Topping

→ p. 113

1 Preheat the oven to 325°F/160°C/gas mark 3.

2 To make the apple compote, combine all the ingredients in a large saucepan.

3 Cover and cook over low heat, stirring occasionally, for about 30 minutes until the apples are tender.

4 Set aside to cool to room temperature.

5 Meanwhile, make the streusel topping. Cream the butter and sugar together in the bowl of a stand mixer.

6 Once creamed, add the flours and mix until just combined and the mixture has a crumbly consistency.

7 Spread the streusel out on a large baking sheet and bake for about 30 minutes until golden.

8 Remove the streusel from the oven and set aside. Maintain the oven temperature at 325°F/160°C/gas mark 3.

9 Place the cooled apple compote in the bottom of a serving dish in a layer at least 1 inch (2.5 cm) deep.

10 Cover the compote with the baked streusel.

11 Place the assembled dessert into the oven for about 10 minutes until heated through.

for the apple compote	for 2	for 6	for 20	for 50
Granny Smith apples, peeled and diced	¾ lb/350 g	1½ lb/700 g	4½ lb/2 kg	11 lb/5 kg
lemon juice	1 tsp	1 tbsp	3 tbsp	½ cup/120 ml
Calvados or apple brandy	1 tsp	1½ tsp	1½ tbsp	4 tbsp
granulated sugar	1 tbsp	2 tbsp	⅓ cup/70 g	¾ cup/175 g
ground cinnamon	⅛ tsp	½ tsp	1½ tsp	1 tbsp
for the streusel				
butter, softened	1 tbsp	6 tbsp	2 sticks/½ lb/225 g	5 sticks/1¼ lb/550 g
confectioners' (icing) sugar	3 tbsp	⅔ cup/70 g	1¾ cups/225 g	5 cups/550 g
all-purpose (plain) flour	3 tbsp	⅔ cup/70 g	1¾ cups/225 g	5 cups/550 g
almond flour	2½ tbsp	⅓ cup/70 g	1⅓ cups/225 g	3¼ cups/550 g

← Staff find a moment to relax in the sunshine of the courtyard.

↑ Comforting dishes, such as the Italian-American classic spaghetti and meatballs, are often eaten on laps or standing up.

→ A late-night meeting held daily after service to plan the next day's menu (overleaf).

The French Laundry

Le Chateaubriand

Location
Paris, France

Established
2006

Head chef
Iñaki Aizpitarte/Laurent Cabut

Sous chef
Agata Felluga

← Sous chef, Agata Felluga takes a break outside the restaurant.

↑ Crushing boxes (top).

↑ Sébastien Chatillon, sommelier, emerges from the old, underground wine cellar (above).

Le Chateaubriand

↑ Looking out on to Avenue Parmentier.

↑ The staff meal is skillfully pulled together
from scraps and leftovers from service, resulting
in popular dishes.

→ After the Hunt (p. 127) plated up (overleaf).

Le Chateaubriand

Le Chateaubriand

Le Chateaubriand is run by a small group of very special, talented people who are intent on doing things differently. It was the first restaurant in Paris to offer high-end food from high-quality produce without the Michelin uniform of white tablecloths and formal service. Its personnel are less interested in stars than in being able to express themselves with complete freedom, and they are very successful at it.

In just a few years, Le Chateaubriand has risen to become one of the most highly regarded restaurants in Paris, but the staff meal still feels very much like eating in someone's home. As in so many Parisian apartments, the kitchen is tiny, with prep spilling over into the dining room; and the food that is cooked is based on whatever they have in the refrigerator. The atmosphere is comfortable and relaxed, a sort of organized chaos with lots of friends and neighbors zipping in and out to say "Hi," which gives it a very intimate vibe. At the same time, there is a focused and creative buzz to the place that keeps it fresh and interesting. That's the magic ingredient, and it comes across in the food.

The menu is based on the best French produce and it changes every day. Because the staff meal is made from the scraps and leftovers, it is always different, too. Paul Boudier, who has been cooking it for the past couple of years, says, "I love doing it because it gives me something to be in charge of, but I also love the spontaneity. I look in the fridge about half an hour before we're going to eat and take it from there." His near-legendary *soupe de pêcheur* (Fisherman's Soup) is made from the fish normally used to make stock; he serves it with a simple mixed herb salad, and everyone gets super-excited about it.

This kind of honest cooking is important. It's refreshing to come across a restaurant that isn't constrained by boundaries, and a lot of creativity comes out of that kind of liberty. It's about always challenging yourself to do better and be more inventive, which of course is what Parisian home cooks do every day.

Sous chef Agata Felluga sums it up perfectly: "I've worked in a lot of Michelin-starred places, but here it's the home-style cooking that's the trick. It's the balance between the perfectionist attitude that you have to have at work, and the need to do something real and solid to share with people: to offer something that makes them happy."

Le Chateaubriand's staff meal is a gentle reminder to everyone that the restaurant's philosophy is deeply rooted in clever, creative home cooking.

Fisherman's Soup

→ p. 130

1   Pour the bouillabaisse or fish soup into a large saucepan or stock pot. Bring to simmer over medium heat.

2   Add the potatoes and simmer for 15 minutes, then add the carrots and onions. Simmer for about 10 minutes until all the vegetables are tender. The vegetables should be covered with liquid; if not, add more boiling water.

3   Add the mussels, fish, cooked chicken, and snow peas (mangetout) to the pan. Cover and cook for another 3–5 minutes, or until the mussels open, the chicken is warm, and the snow peas are tender. Discard any mussels that do not open.

4   Season to taste and serve.

5   For the salad, coarsely chop the herbs and combine with the red onion and seeds. Toss the salad with the vinegar and olive oil, then season and serve.

for the soup	for 2	for 6	for 20	for 50
bouillabaisse or fish soup	scant 1 cup/200 ml	2½ cups/600 ml	7½ cups/1.75 L	4½ qt/4.4 L
new potatoes	5 oz/150 g	1 lb/450 g	3 lb/1.4 kg	7¾ lb/3.5 kg
baby carrots or sliced carrots	3½ oz/100 g	10 oz/300 g	2 lb/900 g	5 lb/2.2 kg
onion, coarsely chopped	4 tbsp	¾ cup/120 g	2 cups/350 g	7½ cups/900 g
mussels, cleaned	5 oz/150 g	1 lb/450 g	3 lb/1.4 kg	7½ lb/3.5 kg
white fish, such as haddock or cod	3 oz/85 g	9 oz/250 g	1 lb 10 oz/750 g	4 lb/1.9 kg
cooked chicken, cut into bite-size chunks	⅓ cup/40 g	1 cup/140 g	3 cups/450 g	2½ lb/1.1 kg
snow peas (mangetout)	1 cup/50 g	3 cups/150 g	7 cups/450 g	2½ lb/1.1 kg

for the herb salad	for 2	for 6	for 20	for 50
fresh mint, leaves and tender stems	1⅓ cups/65 g	2 cups/100 g	6 cups/300 g	15 cups/750 g
fresh cilantro (coriander), leaves and tender stems	1⅔ cups/65 g	2½ cups/100 g	7½ cups/300 g	18 cups/750 g
fresh basil, leaves and tender stems	1⅔ cups/65 g	2½ cups/100 g	7½ cups/300 g	18 cups/750 g
red onions, finely chopped	3 tbsp	¾ cup/120 g	2½ cups/350 g	5½ cups/875 g
seed mix (coriander, sesame, flax, buckwheat)	2 tbsp	½ cup/60 g	1½ cups/180 g	3¾ cups/450 g
sherry vinegar	2 tsp	2 tbsp	6 tbsp	scant 1 cup/250 ml
olive oil	3 tbsp	½ cup/120 ml	1½ cups/350 ml	3¾ cups/900 ml
salt	to taste	to taste	to taste	to taste

After the Hunt

← p. 123–24

Pork roasting times
25 minutes per 1 lb plus 30 minutes
60 minutes per 1kg plus 30 minutes

Roasting times vary depending on
the shape of the roast (joint).

1   Preheat the oven to 425°F/225°C/gas mark 7.

2   Score the skin of the pork for crackling, then sprinkle
    with salt. Place in a roasting pan skin side up. Roast
    for 30 minutes, then turn down the heat to 250°F/120°C/
    gas mark 1 and cook for the roasting time calculated.

3   One hour before the meat is expected to be done, add
    the vegetables and oregano to the roasting pan. Sprinkle
    over the sherry and dot with the butter.

4   Let the roast rest for 45 minutes before carving.

5   In the meantime, make the salad. Wash, dry, and chop
    the lettuce.

6   Make a dressing with the olive oil, lemon, salt, and black
    pepper and pour over the salad.

7   Serve the pork with the vegetables and salad.

for the pork	for 2	for 6	for 20	for 50
pork shoulder roast	–	4½ lb/2 kg	11 lb/5 kg	2 x 13 lb/6 kg
potatoes, large, peeled and cut into wedges	–	5	14	35
turnips, peeled and coasely chopped	–	5	10	25
carrots, peeled and cut into large chunks	–	5	14	35
red onions, cut into wedges	–	3	8	20
tomatoes, coasely chopped	–	4	10	25
fresh oregano, coasely chopped	–	2 tbsp	1 small bunch	2 bunches
sherry vinegar	–	2 tbsp	5 tbsp	¾ cup/175 ml
butter	–	2 tbsp/30 g	6 tbsp/175 g	1¾ sticks/7 oz/200 g

for the salad				
romaine or cos lettuce	–	1 small	2 large	5 large
olive oil	–	6 tbsp	1¼ cups/300 ml	3 cups/750 ml
lemons	–	2	6	15
salt and black pepper	–	to taste	to taste	to taste

Cherry Clafoutis

→ p. 129

1   Preheat the oven to 400°F/200°C/gas mark 6.

2   Line a 5-cup (1.2 L) ovenproof dish with parchment paper. Place the cherries or other fruit in a layer on the bottom.

3   Place the almond meal (ground almonds), confectioners' (icing) sugar, flour, cornstarch (cornflour), and a pinch of salt in the food processor.

4   Mix together the cooled melted butter, eggs, lemon zest, and Calvados, apple brandy or Kirsch.

5   With the motor running, add the liquid ingredients and process until just combined.

6   Spread over the fruit.

7   Bake for 30 minutes or until set.

8   Sprinkle the clafoutis with the brown (demerara) sugar and caramelize the top with a blowtorch or place under a heated broiler (grill) to caramelize. Serve warm.

	for 2	for 6	for 20	for 50
pitted cherries or other soft fruit	–	1½ cups/225 g	–	–
almond meal (ground almonds)	–	1¾ cups/170 g	–	–
confectioners' (icing) sugar	–	1⅓ cups/170 g	–	–
all-purpose (plain) flour	–	1⅓ cups/170 g	–	–
cornstarch (cornflour)	–	⅓ cup/50 g	–	–
butter, melted and cooled	–	4 tbsp/50 g	–	–
eggs	–	3	–	–
zest of lemons	–	2	–	–
Calvados, apple brandy or Kirsch	–	1 tbsp	–	–
light brown (demerara) sugar	–	3 tbsp	–	–

← Cherry clafoutis (p. 128) served with strong
coffee (previous page).

← Fisherman's Soup (p. 126).

↑ The raw ingredients for Fisherman's
Soup (p. 126)

→ 12:30 p.m.: the staff meal serves to remind
people of a restaurant philosophy that is deeply
rooted in home-cooking (overleaf).

Chez Panisse

Location
Berkeley, California, USA

Established
1971

Executive chef
Alice Waters

Head chef
Jérôme Waag

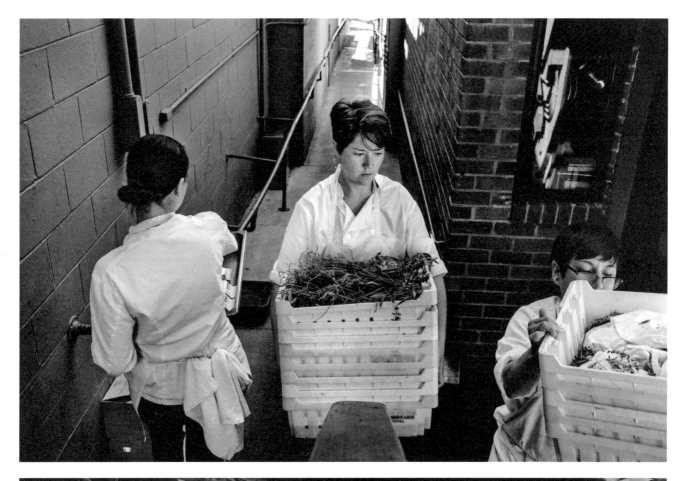

← Shelling broad beans and deciding the menu
(previous page).
← An experimental dessert that was a failure, but
became an unexpected treat.

↑ Staff carrying in produce (top).
↑ The tip tray (above).

→ Squab Torte (p. 143, overleaf).

Chez Panisse

Chez Panisse

When Alice Waters opened her dream restaurant back in the 1970s, it was at a time when organic food, the locavore movement, and regarding your staff as family were still considered to be a bit of a hippie thing. But her food philosophy and belief in treating her staff as she treats her diners have ensured that Chez Panisse has thrived. Everyone talks about it as a place to eat, but if you say you're going for the staff meal, insiders whisper that there's no place like it—it's a legend.

Head chef Jérôme Waag explains: "Since we change the menu daily, we have chosen to serve the staff the same food as the diners. We never know if we are going to serve eight-five or a hundred and there is always extra food. Why cook something different when we only need to cook a few more portions to feed the staff?"

It's a big part of the family meal philosophy that the chefs and cooks get to sit down together to enjoy it. But it also brings them closer to the produce, its provenance, and in the end the dishes it will become after careful preparation in the kitchen. It's not uncommon these days for staff in the best restaurants to taste the menu to improve their knowledge in the dining room, but the openness about the menu planning at Chez Panisse, and the sense of occasion at the staff meal, are completely unique.

It starts with a late afternoon meeting, often outside in the shade of an old tree, where cooks might be shucking beans or peeling potatoes, and they talk about the day's menu. It's like a brainstorming session that makes sure the next service is always better than the previous one, and it demonstrates the understanding, passion, and commitment of the people who work here.

Then, a few hours later, at 8:30 p.m., when the first sitting is over, the entire kitchen downs tools and heads back out to the table to eat. By now, it has been properly set by the interns with a linen cloth, glasses, and silverware, and everyone digs into at least two of the possible three courses on the restaurant menu and a bottle of wine—usually something simple and French to match the food. But it's also a family meal in the truest sense, because of the conversation. It feels very engaged. Discussion of the evening's food is de rigueur, but the talk often veers toward art and politics—this is Berkeley, after all—which adds up to a pretty interesting half hour.

Finally, there is the famous kicker, the little glass of something that everyone is invited to—be it beer, wine, or champagne—to toast the end of each shift. That's the Chez Panisse family meal in a nutshell: it lets your people know they matter.

Summer Vegetable Soup with Pesto

→ p. 145

1   Bring a large saucepan or pot of salted water to the boil. Add the shelled beans, onions, and bouquet garni. Simmer for 30 minutes, until tender.

2   Meanwhile, cut the green beans, zucchini (courgettes), and yellow squash into small pieces, roughly the size of the top of your little finger.

3   Peel and seed the tomatoes. Place the seeds in a strainer (sieve) and strain the juice into the bean broth. Chop the tomatoes.

4   When the beans are tender, drain them, reserving the cooking liquid. Discard the bouquet garni and the onion. Season the liquid to taste with salt. Add the green beans.

5   Bring the liquid back to a simmer, then add the zucchini and squash. When the broth comes to a simmer again, add the beans and the tomatoes. Simmer for 10 minutes, then add the pasta. Simmer for another 10 minutes. If the broth is too dense with vegetables, add a little more water.

6   Meanwhile, make the pesto. Pound the garlic cloves to a paste with a mortar and pestle or puree in a food processor. Add the basil leaves and process to a paste. Add the Parmesan cheese, then drizzle in the olive oil to thin. Let stand in the mortar to serve or turn into a serving bowl.

7   When the pasta is cooked, taste the soup and adjust the seasoning. Let the soup sit for 1 hour, then reheat to serve.

8   Serve in warmed bowls with a generous spoonful of the pesto, accompanied with additional grated Parmesan cheese.

for the soup	for 2	for 6	for 20	for 50
shelled fresh cranberry (borlotti) beans	–	2½ cups/450 g	6½ cups/1.2 kg	15 cups/2.8 kg
yellow onion, quartered	–	1 small	1 large	2 large
bouquet garni	–	1	2	3
green beans (French beans)	–	4 cups/450 g	2½ lb/1.2 kg	5 lb/2.2 kg
zucchini (courgettes)	–	2 medium/450 g	4 medium/900 g	10 medium/2.2 kg
yellow squash	–	2 medium/450 g	4 medium/900 g	10 medium/2.2 kg
tomatoes	–	2	5	12
orzo, conchiglie, or orrechiette pasta	–	4 oz/120 g	10 oz/300 g	1½ lb/750 g
salt and black pepper	–	to taste	to taste	to taste

for the pesto				
garlic cloves	–	6	15	3 heads
basil leaves	–	2 bunches	5 bunches	12 bunches
grated Parmesan cheese	–	4 tbsp/25 g	1½ cups/75 g	2 cups/170 g
extra virgin olive oil	–	½ cup/120 ml	1¼ cups/300 ml	3 cups/750 ml

Squab Torte

← p. 140

The recipe makes one tart for 6 making more than 6 servings, two tarts for 20 and five tarts for 50.

1 First make the dough (pastry). Sift the flour, salt, and sugar into a large bowl. Cut the butter into ½-inch (1-cm) cubes and toss half of it into the flour. Rub in the butter until the mixture resembles coarse bread crumbs.

2 Add the other half of the butter and work into the flour very briefly, leaving it in unincorporated parts. Stir in the ice water with a fork until the flour is evenly moistened.

3 Gather the dough together and divide into two balls. Flatten into two even-size circles and wrap in plastic wrap (clingfilm). Chill for at least 1 hour or up to 24 hours.

4 Meanwhile, make the filling. Season the squabs with salt and black pepper and cut in half. Place the squabs in a large saucepan with the pork skin, mirepoix, bay leaf, and juniper berries and just enough water to cover. Braise over low heat for about 2 hours.

5 When tender, pick out the bones and the juniper berries. Drain and reserve the braising liquid, and set aside.

6 Coarsely chop the meat and return to pan. Add the reserved braising liquid and let simmer until the mixture is soft and thickened. Set aside to cool.

7 Preheat the oven to 400°F/200°C/gas mark 6.

8 Wilt the greens, add the chopped garlic, and set aside. Place the sliced onions and thyme in a skillet or frying pan and cook over low heat until soft and translucent. Set aside.

9 Roll each dough circle into a 12-inch (30-cm) circle about ⅛-inch (4-mm) thick. Layer the fillings onto the dough one at a time. Spread a layer of the caramelized onions to cover the surface of the dough. Continue by adding a layer of greens and then a layer of the braised squab.

10 Top the layers with the second round of dough and pinch the edges of the pastry closed. Make 8 small incisions on the top and brush the pastry with a mixture of egg yolk and cream. Place in the oven for 45 minutes until golden brown.

for the dough (pastry)	for 2	for 6	for 20	for 50
all-purpose (plain) flour	–	1 cup/120 g	2 cups/250 g	5 cups/625 g
salt	–	¼ tsp	½ tsp	1¼ tsp
superfine (caster) sugar	–	pinch	¼ tsp	¾ tsp
butter	–	6 tbsp/85 g	1½ sticks/6 oz/170 g	3¾ sticks/15 oz/425 g
ice water	–	4 tbsp	5 tbsp	1 cup/250 ml
egg yolk	–	1	1	3 yolks
cream	–	1 tbsp	1 tbsp	3 tbsp

for the filling	for 2	for 6	for 20	for 50
whole squab	–	2	4	10
fresh pork skin	–	4 oz/120 g	8 oz/240 g	1 lb 5 oz/600 g
carrots, celery, and yellow onion, diced to make mirepoix	–	1 lb 2 oz/500 g	2¼ lb/1 kg	5½ lb/2.5 kg
bay leaf	–	1	2	5
juniper berries	–	10	20	50
mixed greens: amaranth, borage, green chard, arugula (rocket)	–	2 lb/900 g	4 lb/1.8 kg	10 lb/4.5 kg
yellow onions, sliced	–	4	8	20
garlic cloves, finely chopped	–	3	6	15
fresh thyme sprigs	–	5	10	25
salt and black pepper	–	to taste	to taste	to taste

Champagne Gelatin (Jelly)

1 Put the first measure of water into a saucepan and stir in the sugar. Heat over low heat, stirring occasionally, until the sugar dissolves. Do not boil. Set aside.

2 Put the second measure of water into a small saucepan. Sprinkle over the gelatin so that it is absorbed by the water. If necessary, add a little more water.

3 Warm the gelatin over low heat until it melts. Do not stir. Do not let it boil. Add a small amount of the warmed sugar syrup to the gelatin, then add all the gelatin back to the sugar syrup.

4 Pour in the champagne. Strain into an 8 x 8-inch (20 x 20-cm) baking pan for 6 servings or two 9 x 13-inch (22 x 33-cm) pans for 20 servings. Refrigerate for about 4 hours until set.

	for 2	for 6	for 20	for 50
water	–	⅔ cup/150 ml	2 cups/500 ml	–
superfine (caster) sugar	–	½ cup/100 g	1½ cups/300 g	–
water	–	2 tbsp	½ cup/120 ml	–
powdered gelatin	–	2 tsp	4 tbsp	–
champagne	–	2 cups/500 ml	6¾ cups/1.6 L	–

Raspberry Sherbet (Sorbet)

1 Put the sugar and water into a saucepan over medium-low heat. Let the sugar dissolve, stirring occasionally. When the sugar is dissolved, turn up the heat and bring to a boil. Cool to room temperature, then chill completely.

2 Meanwhile, puree the raspberries through a food mill or in a food processor. Pass through a fine strainer (sieve) to remove the seeds.

3 Stir the chilled syrup into the puree.

4 Taste and add a few drops of Kirsch, if liked. Chill thoroughly. Freeze in an ice cream machine following the manufacturer's instructions.

	for 2	for 6	for 20	for 50
granulated sugar	–	⅓ cup/60 g	1½ cups/350 g	–
water	–	scant ½ cup/100 ml	1¼ cups/300 ml	–
raspberries	–	2½ cups/300 g	7⅓ cups/900 g	–
Kirsch (optional)	–	to taste	to taste	–

← Katri Foster and Josh Heller (previous pages).

← Taking a break from cooking, the staff
eat outside.

↑ Amy Dencler enjoying a last minute bite.

Maison Pic

Location
Valence, France

Established
1889

Head chef
Anne-Sophie Pic

Executive chef
Fabien Zucconi

← Fine dining is all in the details (previous pages).　↑ A lesson in how to truss a bird.　→ Chef, Xavier Jarry trussing a bird.

Maison Pic

It's hard to imagine that Maison Pic was once just a simple roadside tavern offering rest and sustenance to weary travelers crossing France. The fairly nondescript suburbs of Valence gradually grew up around it, but when you enter the glittering glass doors to the courtyard, it's an Alice-down-the-rabbit-hole moment, where you end up in a world of dazzling luxury.

Here are two restaurants: one a classic French bistro that is everything you could wish for, and the other a historic three-Michelin-starred restaurant. Both are now run by Anne-Sophie Pic, and the pressure is really on her because the restaurant has had its stars forever. Her grandfather, André Pic, first earned the restaurant three stars in 1934 and her father, Jacques Pic, retained them when he took over. When Anne-Sophie arrived in 1992, she was just twenty-three years old. Her father died three months later and it was a lot to take on for such a young chef. In 1995 the restaurant lost its third star and so began her campaign to win it back. In 2007 she triumphed, going on to win the title of Veuve Clicquot World's Best Female Chef in 2011.

This single-minded focus on creating the perfect restaurant experience has always been a means of honoring her family, but in 2012 Anne-Sophie began to radically rethink their approach to staff meals, too. With so many people to feed—they now number more than a hundred—the primary goal had always been to provide fresh, nutritious, and balanced meals, but she wanted to find ways to encourage friendships to develop within the team, too.

"We are trying to reorganize the kitchen with a special place for the staff meal in it," Anne-Sophie explains. "I don't like the fact that everyone wants to eat near where they are working at the moment. I would like everyone to have lunch together, but it is difficult because we are so many."

The team, however, have embraced her vision with gusto, some of them making space and time for themselves in the most ingenious of ways. There is a hidden elevator that connects the restaurant to the wine cellar, and here the sommeliers have set up a small "dining room," where they eat and taste wine. It's almost like a speakeasy from the 1930s, a secret club where they go to enhance their craft and socialize. And while not everyone has access to the wine cellar, special rituals are slowly emerging as part of Maison Pic's culture. The pastry kitchen, for example, now saves any of their extravagant, hand-painted cakes and pastries that are left over and gives them to other kitchen staff as a welcomde afternoon treat.

"Focusing more attention on this area reflected immediately on the atmosphere and relationships between staff. It is a great improvement for the team," says Anne-Sophie. "It doesn't matter where you go to have it, the pay-off is a meal among friends."

Chicken Liver Salad

1 Rinse the chicken livers and trim away any green parts or white stringy pieces. Divide into bite-size pieces, if necessary. Pat dry on paper towels and refrigerate until required.

2 For the croutons, preheat the oven to 400°F/200°C/gas mark 6. Tear the bread into small pieces and put onto a baking sheet in a layer no more than ½ inch (1 cm) thick. Sprinkle over a little olive oil and toss to lightly coat the bread. Bake in the oven for about 5 minutes or until golden brown, stirring occasionally. Remove from the oven and set aside.

3 For the salad, tear the salad greens (leaves) into bite-size pieces, rinse and dry. Place in a large bowl and set aside until required.

4 Place the vinegar in a bowl and whisk in the mustard to combine. Gradually add the oil while whisking to emulsify the dressing. Season to taste with salt and black pepper.

5 Place the oil in a large skillet or frying pan over medium-high heat. When hot, season the chicken livers and add to the pan. Do not overcrowd the pan or the livers will not brown. If necessary, use several pans or cook the livers in batches. Cook, turning frequently, until the livers are brown on the outside but still pink on the inside. They should not appear bloody.

6 In the meantime, toss the salad with the vinaigrette and divide among serving plates, then divide the livers among the plates.

7 Deglaze the pan with the port and spoon over the salads. Top with the croutons and serve immediately.

for the livers	for 2	for 6	for 20	for 50
chicken livers	6 oz/175 g	1 lb 2 oz/500 g	3¼ lb/1.5 kg	–
Port wine	2 tbsp	4 tbsp	¾ cup/175 ml	–
olive oil	1 tbsp	2 tbsp	6 tbsp	–
salt and black pepper	to taste	to taste	to taste	–

for the croutons				
stale bread, slices	1–2	2–3	10–12	–
olive oil, to coat				–

for the salad				
salad greens (leaves)	2 cups/60 g	12 cups/175 g	1 lb 5 oz/600 g	–
vinegar	1½ tsp	1 tbsp	3½ tbsp	–
Dijon mustard	½ tsp	1 tsp	1 tbsp	–
good quality olive oil	5 tsp	3 tbsp	⅔ cup/150 ml	–
salt and black pepper	to taste	to taste	to taste	–

Roast Chicken with Apple and Onion Confit and Pommes Mousseline

→ p. 156

1 First make the broth. Place all of the ingredients in a large saucepan with enough water to cover. Bring to a simmer and cook 30 minutes. Strain, retaining the broth and discarding the vegetables and aromatics. Set aside.

2 Season the chicken inside and out with salt and black pepper. Place half an apple inside each chicken.

3 Place the oil in a pressure cooker and add the butter. Melt over medium heat, then brown the chicken well on all sides. Remove the chicken and skim off the fat.

4   Add the onions to the pan and cook until softened, then add the remaining apple. Add the cider to the pan. Bring to a boil and reduce by half. Strain the apple and onion from the cider and set to one side. Return the cider to the pan.

5   Return the chicken to the pan with the cider and cover with the broth (stock). Cover the pressure cooker and close securely. Set the regulator valve to 1. When the steam starts to escape, cook for 14 minutes. Reduce the pressure valve very gently but do not open it completely or the fibers of the meat will be damaged. Keep to one side.

6   For the *pommes mousseline*, wash and peel the potatoes and cut into 2-inch (5-cm) pieces. Place in a large saucepan, cover with cold water, and add salt to taste. Bring to a boil, then reduce the heat and simmer for 20 minutes or until tender when pierced with a knife. Drain well, then return to the hot pan to steam dry.

7   Meanwhile, infuse the milk with the spices for 20 minutes. Strain the milk to remove the spices, then add the butter to the milk to melt.

8   Push the hot potatoes through a ricer or food mill. Stir in the hot milk and butter to make a soft mash. Adjust the seasoning with salt and additional butter, if desired. Cover and set aside.

9   Remove the chicken to a carving board. Reduce the chicken sauce, if necessary, to make a lightly syrupy sauce.

10 Carve the chicken, transfer to a platter, and serve with the apple and onion confit and sauce.

	for 2	for 6	for 20	for 50
organic roasting chicken	–	1 x 4 lb/1.8 kg	5 x 3 lb/1.4 kg	–
crips, sweet apples, peeled, cored, and quartered	–	2	6	–
vegetable oil	–	1 tbsp	4 tbsp	–
butter	–	4 tbsp/50 g	1½ sticks/6 oz/180 g	–
onions, thinly sliced	–	1	3	–
dry cider	–	3 cups/750 ml	10 cups/2.5 L	–
salt and black pepper	–	to taste	to taste	–

for the broth (stock)

	for 2	for 6	for 20	for 50
small carrots, chopped	–	2	6	–
onion, coarsely chopped	–	1	3	–
leek, cut into ½-inch (1-cm) slices	–	½	2	–
celery sticks, cut into ½-inch (1-cm) slices	–	1	3	–
whole cloves	–	5	15	–
white peppercorns	–	to taste	to taste	–
water	–	8½ cups/2 L	6⅓ qt/6 L	–

for the pommes mousseline

	for 2	for 6	for 20	for 50
old, floury potatoes	–	1½ lb/700 g	5½ lb/2.5 kg	–
sea salt	–	1 tbsp	3 tbsp	–
milk	–	⅔ cup/150 ml	2 cups/600 ml	–
whole star anise	–	1	3	–
cinnamon stick	–	1	3	–
ground cassia	–	to taste	to taste	–
whole coriander seeds	–	3	9	–
pink peppercorns	–	10	30	–
slightly salted butter	–	4 tbsp/50 g	1¼ sticks/5 oz/150 g	–

Chocolate Mousse

1 Chop the chocolate into small pieces no larger than peas. Put into a heatproof bowl.

2 Put the yolks in a small bowl. Set aside.

3 Put the egg whites in a clean, grease-free metal or glass bowl. Beat the whites and when they start to peak, whisk in the sugar a little at a time. The mixture should be glossy. Do not overbeat or they will be difficult to fold into the chocolate. Set aside.

4 Heat the cream to boiling in the saucepan or microwave. Immediately pour it over the chocolate and stir to melt the chocolate evenly. If it does not melt completely, heat in the microwave on 10-second bursts, using the defrost setting, or place the bowl over a saucepan of simmering water and stir until smooth.

5 Stir the yolks into the chocolate mixture. Using a metal spoon, stir in one spoonful of whites to loosen the mixture, then carefully fold in the remaining whites, being careful not to knock out any air. Let the mousse stand in the bowl to serve (clean the edges of the bowl) or spoon into individual ramekins.

6 Cover with plastic wrap (clingfilm) but do not let it touch the mousse. Refrigerate for at least 2 hours before serving.

	for 2	for 6	for 20	for 50
bittersweet (dark) chocolate	3 oz/80 g	7 oz/200 g	1 lb 7 oz/650 g	–
egg yolks	1	2	7	–
egg whites	1½	4	1¾	–
superfine (caster) sugar	1½ tbsp	⅓ cup/60 g	1 cup/200 g	–
light (single) cream	2 tbsp	6 tbsp	1¼ cups/300 ml	–

↑ Chocolate Mousse (p. 160).

Maison Pic

← Croque monsieur being enjoyed by a pastry chef.

↑ Leftover, hand-painted cakes from the pastry station (top).

↑ Practicing the art of French cooking (above).

→ Goodfellas: Sommeliers Sébastien Schaer, Patrice Fournier, and Denis Bertrand eat in the wine cellar.

Mugaritz

Location
Errenteria, Spain

Established
1998

Executive chef
Andoni Luis Aduriz

Head chef
Julieta Caruso

← Too big to go any other way, the paella is carried outside and then into the staff dining room.

↑ Javi Vergara is the eternal joker.

→ The Mugaritz staff meal is characterized by traditional Spanish dishes, such as this tortilla, and regional classics, such as this salt cod dish (overleaf).

Mugaritz

"Family meal is the most important station at Mugaritz," begins the in-house recipe book, followed by the advice: "Most important of all is to cook with your heart and your soul."

It is so important, in fact, that this recipe book has been created in collaboration with a nutritionist, following clear guiding principles: cream and butter are not to be used, dishes should be low in salt, and there must always be three courses in typically Spanish fashion, such as a soup or salad to start, fish, meat, or eggs forming the main protein, and fruit or yogurt for dessert.

That says it all, because the family meal at Mugaritz is like few others, with as much focus placed on its creation as on the dishes being served to guests in the dining room. When head chef Julieta Caruso sources produce, for example, whether from local suppliers or grown in the on-site garden, it's exactly the same for staff meals as for paying diners. And both menus are based on a scientific approach to meal planning supported by serious research. In the dining room it's about creativity, for family meal it's about nutrition. For both, the approach is rigorous and precise. "At Mugaritz you're learning every day," Julieta says. "I really appreciate that."

The family meal station is an essential part of a chef's training at Mugaritz, mirroring the essence of the restaurant experience. Two stagiaires work it for one whole month, during which time they will cook all the family meals by following the recipe book to the letter. It sounds rigid, but it is actually a very strong way of embedding the discipline and philosophy of the Mugaritz kitchen in the general mind-set, and the message is very positive: Staff must be cared for properly and given the same nutritional attention as any of the diners.

In return, they have a place to call their own, a staff dining room that was built after a fire in 2010. Linked to the restaurant kitchen and offices by a back staircase, there is nothing glamorous about this room, but its utilitarian qualities are closely linked to the culinary heritage of the region. Designed to look like the *sidrerias* (local cider taverns) that are dotted throughout the hills of the region, it has a pull-down table attached to the wall with simple cafeteria-style wooden benches that suit the mostly regional food: *bacalao ajoarriero* (salt cod pounded together with potatoes and garlic), *alubias con sacramentos* (white beans stewed with scraps of pork and sausages), or the Sunday paella based on a pan of rice large enough to feed a small village and which lends a festive air to the end of the week.

This is Spain, after all, and no matter how serious a place is, you can't escape the inherently convivial nature—or should that be nurture—of breaking bread together.

Lentil Stew with Pork Ribs

1   Put half the oil in a Dutch oven or casserole dish over medium heat.

2   Season the pork ribs with salt and black pepper, then brown on all sides in the hot oil. Set aside on a plate. Pour off any excess fat from the pan, leaving a little behind for the vegetables.

3   Put the onions in the pan and cook over medium-low heat until softened, then stir in the carrots and leeks. Cook the vegetables until softened but not colored.

4   Add the lentils and the browned ribs to the pan and add cold water to cover. Bring to simmer, then cover and cook over low heat for 50 minutes or until the lentils are soft.

5   Put the remaining oil in a skillet or frying pan over low heat. Add the sliced garlic and cook, stirring, until pale golden. Pour over the lentils.

6   Season the lentils with Spanish paprika and salt. Serve hot.

	for 2	for 6	for 20	for 50
olive oil	2 tbsp	6 tbsp	scant 1 cup/200 ml	–
pork ribs	7 oz/200 g	1¼ lb/600 g	4½ lb/2 kg	–
yellow onions, finely diced	⅓ cup/60 g	1 cup/175 g	3½ cups/575 g	–
carrots, diced small	⅓ cup/60 g	1¼ cups/175 g	4 cups/575 g	–
leeks, diced small	⅔ cup/60 g	2 cups/175 g	6½ cups/575 g	–
green lentils, washed	1¼ cups/250 g	4 cups/750 g	12½ cups/2.5 kg	–
garlic cloves, sliced	2	6	20	–
Spanish paprika	pinch	large pinch	1 tsp	–
salt and black pepper	to taste	to taste	to taste	–

Paella

→ p. 180

1 Remove the shells from the shrimp (prawns) and devein them, if necessary. Save the shells for making fish broth (stock).

2 Put half the olive oil in a skillet or frying pan and stir in the onions. Cook for 5 minutes over medium-low heat until starting to soften. Add the red and green bell peppers and continue to cook until the vegetables are soft. Stir in the garlic and cook for another minute.

3 Add the saffron threads and cook until the vegetables are lightly carmelized. Add the tomato and cook for another 5 minutes.

4 In the meantime, make the picada. Place the almonds, garlic, and parsley in a food processor. Process to a fine paste. Drizzle over the olive oil and process to combine. Place in a serving bowl and set aside until required.

5 In a separate skillet or frying pan, heat the remaining oil over medium heat. Cook the shrimp until lightly browned and nearly cooked through.

6 Add the rice to the vegetables and cook for 5 minutes while stirring. Warm the fish broth (stock), then add to the vegetables. Bring to a simmer. Season with salt and black pepper, then cover and cook over low heat for 5 minutes. Add the shrimp. Cook for another 5 minutes.

7 To make the aioli, whisk the yolks in a small bowl and slowly drizzle in the olive oil while whisking. Whisk in the garlic and season with salt. Place in a serving bowl and set aside.

8 Turn off the heat under the paella and let it rest for 5 minutes. Serve with the picada and the aioli.

for the paella	for 2	for 6	for 20	for 50
large raw shell-on shrimp (prawns)	9 oz/250 g	1 lb 10 oz/750 g	5½ lb/2.5 kg	–
olive oil	2 tbsp	4 tbsp	scant 1 cup/200 ml	–
yellow onion, finely diced	⅔ cup/100 g	1¼ cups/200 g	4 cups/650 g	–
red bell pepper, finely diced	½ large	2	5½	–
green bell pepper, finely diced	½ large	2	5½	–
garlic cloves, crushed	2	6	18	–
saffron threads	small pinch	large pinch	3 large pinches	–
tomatoes, seeded and finely chopped	1 cup/200 g	3 cups/600 g	4½ lb/2 kg	–
Spanish paella (Bomba) rice or risotto rice	1 cup/200 g	3 cups/600 g	10 cups/2 kg	–
fish broth (stock)	2–3 cups/500–700 ml	6–9 cups/1.4–2.2 L	5–8 qt/4.5–7.3 L	–
salt and black pepper	to taste	to taste	to taste	–

for the picada				
almonds, toasted	3 tbsp	½ cup/60 g	1⅓ cups/200 g	–
garlic cloves	½	1	3	–
parsley	½ cup/30 g	1 cup/60 g	3 cups/200 g	–
olive oil	4 tbsp	scant ½ cup/100 ml	1½ cups/330 ml	–

for the aioli				
egg yolks	1	1	3	–
olive oil	4 tbsp	4 tbsp	scant 1 cup/200 ml	–
garlic cloves, crushed	1	1	3	–
salt	to taste	to taste	to taste	–

Flan

→ p. 177

1 Put the milk and vanilla bean(s) in a saucepan over medium heat and warm until the milk begins to steam. Turn off the heat.

2 Put the egg yolk and whole eggs into a bowl with the sugar and stir to combine. Try not to make the mixture frothy.

3 Remove the vanilla beans (pods) from the milk and rinse, then dry well. Store in the sugar jar.

4 Slowly pour the warm milk onto the eggs while stirring. Pass the mixture through a strainer (sieve) into a heat-proof bowl.

5 Preheat the oven to 325°F/160°C/gas mark 3.

6 Place ramekins in the oven on a baking sheet to warm.

7 Put the sugar for the caramel in a heavy saucepan. Cover with ½ inch (1 cm) water. Place over medium-low heat and warm, stirring occasionally, until the sugar dissolves completely.

8 Turn up the heat to high and watch the sugar closely until it turns a golden brown. Do not stir. Using an oven mitt (glove) to protect your hand and arm, and very carefully pour the caramelized sugar into the ramekins. Swirl the ramekins to coat.

9 Place the ramekins in a roasting pan. Pour boiling water into the roasting pan so that it comes halfway up the sides of the ramekins. Pour the custard mixture into the ramekins. Cover each ramekin with foil.

10 Place the pan in the center of the oven and bake until the custard is nearly set but still slightly jiggly when the ramekin is given a little shake. Remove the ramekins from the bain-marie and let the flans sit for at least 30 minutes. Refrigerate until cold.

11 To serve, run a knife around the edge of each flan. Invert onto individual plates.

	for 2	for 6	for 20	for 50
whole (full-fat) milk	scant 1 cup/200 ml	3 cups/700 ml	7½ cups/1.75 L	–
vanilla beans (pods)	1	2	5	–
egg yolks	1	2	5	–
eggs	2	6	15	–
superfine (caster) sugar	4 tbsp	¾ cup/150 g	scant 2 cups/375 g	–

for the caramel

granulated sugar	¾ cup/150 g	2½ cups/500 g	6 cups/1.2 kg	–

← 12 Noon: staff meal dining room, inspired by local cider houses (previous page).
← Paella (p. 175).

↑ Leire Etxaide, forager, chef and a member of the creative team (top).

↑ 5:01 p.m.: Nicolas Boise, sommelier (above).

Noma

Location
Copenhagen, Denmark

Established
2004

Head chef
René Redzepi

↑ Cooking on the ceramic barbecue.

→ Leftovers from the restaurant, such as this cucumber, form the basis of the dishes served at the staff meal.

→ Tom Halpin gives pastry chef Rosio Sanchez a short massage for sore shoulders. take time out to relax (overleaf).

→ Guilty pleasures: Rory Cowcher's homemade ketchup has reached cult status inside Noma's sleek, staff dining room (p. 188).

STAFF CUCUMBER 10/11/11 '06

Noma

Breakfast at Noma seems a fairly ordinary affair. Usually it's something like a bowl of oatmeal (porridge), which you can eat standing up. But occasionally it offers a glimpse into another world, as when a German chef makes his famous dumplings.

Yann's recipe for breakfast dumplings with cucumber in fresh cream and dill was created by his great-grandmother in the 1920s, and passed down through the family until it eventually reached him. It's a simple sort of sustenance, but one that perfectly reflects the sense of time and place that is so essential to Noma's philosophy of food and thus easily digested during the staff meal.

Here it's not just the ingredients and their provenance, but the stories behind them that give the dishes soul. The radical policy of letting chefs take plates to table, for example, has been fundamental in training them to be able to speak about the food they are serving, to share experiences, and to connect them to the diner on a deeper level. And giving stagiaires free rein to cook dishes for the staff meal that come from their roots enables them to express a stronger sense of who they are.

Like most chefs, Noma's have their guilty pleasures, among them the desire for ketchup on certain dishes. But René is not a fan and had effectively banned it from the restaurant until one day a young stagiaire cooked his grandmother's recipe for it. It went down so well with everyone, including René, that it has been made regularly ever since, decanted into empty wine bottles that take pride of place in the staff dining room.

There are approximately twenty-two nationalities working at Noma, and getting a glimpse of their culture through their food adds an intimacy to the staff meal that is hard to replicate in any other way. "René wants and expects staff meal to be 'the main meal of our lives,'" explains chef Beau Clugston. "It has to be something delicious, cooked with patience and care, but it also has to be something that chefs are committed to. It's more than just dinner."

The staff meal has now been integrated into the restaurant culture to the extent that when the restaurant was refurbished in 2011, and moved upstairs next to the test kitchen, it literally went public. Everyone who eats at Noma gets a tour of the test kitchen and the herb garden and a sneak preview of what is coming up on a mood board, but now they get an insider's glimpse of the staff space, too.

Here you have it: A staff dining room that is better-looking than many restaurants with sleek Danish-designed tables and ergonomic dining chairs, and a staff meal that is richly diverse and comparatively expensive. But this is Noma, and living the philosophy is all part of the reward for staff and diners alike.

Flour Dumplings with Cucumbers and Cream

1   Peel and seed the cucumbers. Slice thinly with a mandolin, being careful to keep your fingers well away from the sharp blade or slice as thinly as possible with a sharp knife.

2   Put the sliced cucumber in a colander and sprinkle with the salt and sugar. Mix well and let drain for at least 30 minutes.

3   In the meantime, make the dumplings. Sift the flour and salt into the mixing bowl of a standard mixer. Stir in the milk, water, and eggs. Add the nutmeg. Beat at a high speed until the mixture is well combined and bubbly.

4   Fill a large saucepan halfway with water and season well with salt. Bring to a boil, then reduce the heat so that the water simmers gently.

5   Using two spoons of the same size, form quenelles from the dumpling mixture and drop them into the water. Simmer for 10 minutes or until the dumplings rise to the top of the pan and feel firm to the touch.

6   Remove with a slotted spoon and drain on a clean dish towel.

7   Rinse the cucumber and drain away any excess liquid. Pat dry with paper towels.

8   Put the cucumber in a bowl and stir in the cream and dill. Season with vinegar and black pepper.

9   Serve the dumplings hot with the cold salad.

for the dumplings	for 2	for 6	for 20	for 50
all-purpose (plain) flour	1 cup/120 g	3 cups/360 g	7½ cups/900 g	–
salt	large pinch	½ tsp	1¼ tsp	–
whole (full-fat) milk	2 tbsp	scant ½ cup/100 ml	1 cup/250 ml	–
water	2 tbsp	scant ½ cup/100 ml	1 cup/250 ml	—
eggs, beaten	1	3	8	—
ground nutmeg	small pinch	¼ tsp	½ tsp	—

for the cucumber salad	for 2	for 6	for 20	for 50
cucumbers	1 lb/450 g	3¼ lb/1.5 kg	8 lb/3.7 kg	–
superfine (caster) sugar	1 tsp	1 tbsp	2½ tbsp	—
heavy (double) cream	2 tbsp	scant ½ cup/100 ml	1 cup/250 ml	—
fresh dill, leaves and tender stems	3 tbsp	⅓ cup/30 g	1½ cups/75 g	—
salt	1 tsp	1 tbsp	2½ tbsp	—
vinegar	to taste	to taste	to taste	—
black pepper	to taste	to taste	to taste	—

Chocolate Chip Cookies

→ p. 193

1 Beat the butter and sugar together until pale and fluffy.

2 Add the beaten eggs gradually while beating.

3 Sift together the flour, baking soda, salt, cocoa powder then fold into the butter/sugar mixture using a large metal spoon.

4 Fold in the chocolate chips.

5 Chill the mixture for 1 hour.

6 Preheat the oven to 325°F/160°C/gas mark 3.

7 Line the baking sheets with parchment paper.

8 Divide the cookie mixture into equal-sized balls. Bake in the center of the preheated oven for 15–20 minutes.

9 Let stand on the baking sheet for one minute then remove with a spatula to a wire rack to cool completely. Store in an airtight container.

	for 2	for 6	for 20	for 50
unsalted butter	–	7 tbsp/100 g	1¾ sticks/7 oz/200 g	4½ sticks/1 lb 2 oz/500 g
superfine (caster) sugar	–	¾ cup/150 g	1½ cups/300 g	3¾ cups/750 g
eggs, beaten	–	1	2	5
all-purpose (plain) flour	–	1 cup/125 g	2 cups/250 g	5 cups/600 g
baking soda (bicarbonate of soda)	–	1 tsp	2 tsp	3 tbsp
salt	–	pinch	¼ tsp	¾ tsp
unsweetened cocoa powder	–	⅓ cup/35 g	¾ cup/70 g	2 cups/175 g
chocolate chips	–	⅔ cup/100 g	1¼ cups/200 g	2¾ cups/500 g

Brownies

→ p. 193

1   In a double boiler or heatproof bowl set over but not touching, a saucepan of simmering water, melt the butter and chocolate. Stir to combine. Remove the bowl from the water and let cool to room temperature.

2   Preheat the oven to 325°F/160°C/gas mark 3. Line the baking pan with parchment paper. For 6, use an 8-inch (20-cm) square pan; for 20, use an 9 x 13-inch (22 x 33-cm) pan. (For 50 brownies, bake them in batches.)

3   Whisk the eggs in a stand mixture until they are pale and a thick ribbon falls from the beaters. Gradually whisk in the sugar.

4   Using a large metal spoon, fold the chocolate mixture into the egg mixture.

5   Mix the flour and salt together and sift over the chocolate mixture. Fold in gently, then fold in the nuts.

6   Turn into the prepared pan and bake in the center of the oven for about 25 minutes until a toothpick or wooden skewer inserted in the center comes out with a few moist crumbs attached.

7   Cool in the pan on a wire rack. Cut into squares to serve.

	for 2	for 6	for 20	for 50
unsalted butter	–	5 tbsp/75 g	10 tbsp/150 g	–
semisweet (dark) chocolate (70% cocoa solids)	–	6 oz/175 g	12 oz/350 g	–
eggs, beaten	–	2	4	–
dark brown (muscovado) sugar	–	⅔ cup/160 g	1½ cups/320 g	–
all-purpose (plain) flour	–	½ cup/60 g	1 cup/125 g	–
salt	–	pinch	¼ tsp	–
walnuts, chopped	–	½ cup/60 g	1 cup/125 g	–

↑ Noma's team consider the daily staff meal "the main meal of our lives."

→ James Cross grabs a plate.

↑ James Cross moves between the kitchen and the outside barbecue.

→ Breakfast at Noma is a simple, yet delicious, affair.

Osteria Francescana

Location
Modena, Italy

Established
1995

Head chef
Massimo Bottura

Creative team
Davide Di Fabio
Takahiko Kondo
Yoji Tokuyoshi

↑ From left to right: Massimo Bottura, Takahiko Kondo, Davide Di Fabio, and Yoji Tokuyoshi (top).

→ A height chart in the old kitchen.

→ Yoji Tokuyoshi (overleaf).

NO.1 FRANK! SARDELLÒ '93 NO1!

DIO

IMMAGINE 192 cm STEFANY 210 BALBO No.1!

.08 21:05
.10.08. 19.55
31.10.08 .19:25
MATTE
BUDDY JACK MIKE MICCA MARCO DE ROMA IVANO (Icar) LEO 22anni Ancona MARCO ME (non da Roma) DAVIDE
LEO FRANCI Treviso
ANGELO ENRICO (Ancona)
BRASIL Jhon Jack Adam CERVI
GILBERTO DO BRAZIL MAURO MARCE manuel sala ALLE ALBA MAX BEPPE 13-10-07 Salvato
Luca Mirandoli DEL!! Donny panettie Bardagian Miho SAMIR
Toto (BILLY Lallo AZIZ Zanna FOX Todhi Yogi (DOTTORE) PIERINO
RICKY Bordon ALE INGRID TAKA BELLANTE 210 LUCIII!
GRAZIELA 25/3/2011 AGATA PACCIANI Federica SIMO 1.7
Luca Testina NIKOLAS YURI
FACIOCINO F!! 16/9/2010 SANDRINO NIKO
Nivato TATIANA SILVANA KAMAL CECIA SANDE
ANA BIANCHI 03/ /2011 BARBARA VALENTINA SHERLYN
Notasha 16/02/09 ALEXA Alexa CIAO
WILLY 02/12/ ALEXA
SAN ALEXA FIERA VIRG

Osteria Francescana

When the Osteria Francescana got its third Michelin star in 2011, sommelier Beppe Palmieri was so proud he had three stars tattooed on his inner forearm. That tells you a lot about how the staff feel about this restaurant and their mentor, Massimo Bottura.

In Italy it's easy to become part of the family, and here at Francescana those rites of passage usually take place over the staff meal. Plastered with posters of Massimo's beloved team Inter Milan, the staff dining room feels very much like the soccer clubs you find in so many Mediterranean cities. Here he holds court in a totally overdramatic way, but at the same time he's immensely warm and funny. This is the wonderful thing about the Francescana staff meal: rarely do you hear anyone talking about work. Mostly the conversation is about soccer scores, current events, bad haircuts, and so on. What matters most is for the entire staff—chefs, waiters, maître, interns, chef Bottura, and sometimes his wife Lara, who does the flower arrangements among many other things—to be sitting at one table together for lunch and dinner. Around this table they are all equals, just having a meal.

This is a staff meal that is deeply entrenched in good old-fashioned camaraderie, and a strong sense that you're at home both physically and mentally. Situated in a rambling old house in the heart of the old city of Modena, the restaurant takes over almost an entire block with the office, kitchen, wine cellar, and dining room in one part, the prep kitchen, bakery, pasta making, and staff dining room in another, and storage opposite. It means the street is always busy with the team's comings and goings, so the team are deeply connected to the local community. Because of that, no matter where the staff come from, they almost have to become Italian to work here. The staff meal is part of that integration process.

This is a place where the chefs don't just learn how to make the dishes; they must live and breathe them. Massimo learned to cook from a local woman named Lydia, who lives twenty minutes from Modena and is an expert tortellini maker. Now, once a week the team go and prepare tortellini with her: tiny, delicate ones for the contemporary restaurant menu, and the larger, heartier kind for staff meals. Lydia's countryside neighbors come and join in, and the occasion turns into one of those cheerful gatherings that are so typical of Italy and always involve honest, unpretentious food.

"Ragù is life. I can't live without pasta," says Andrea, one of the floor staff, admitting a fondness for other staff meal regulars, such as pizza, *bollito misto* and rabbit cacciatore, as well as Japanese chefs Yoji and Taka's occasional yakitori. But the spirit of the occasion transcends the food. The meal is a reminder that they are all in it together. All for one and one for all, and nothing could be more Italian than that.

Spaghetti with Mussels

1   Put the mussels in a Dutch oven or casserole dish over medium-high heat. Stir with a spoon from time to time to help the mussels near the top of the pan to reach the bottom. When the mussels have opened wide, drain in a colander, making sure to catch the juice from the mussels in a pan. Discard any mussels that are cracked or have not opened.

2   Remove the mussels from their shells and set aside.

3   Place a large saucepan three-quarters full with salted water on to boil for the spaghetti.

4   Put the half of the olive oil in a skillet or frying pan, over medium heat and add the garlic and parsley. When the garlic starts to brown, add the wine and tomatoes. Cook for about 4 minutes or until the tomatoes start to soften.

5   Pour the mussel liquid into the pan, being careful to leave any gritty sediment behind. Bring to a simmer and cook until reduced by half. Add the cooked mussels and keep warm.

6   Cook the spaghetti in the boiling salted water until nearly done (*al dente*), then drain and return to the pan with a little of the cooking water. Whisk in the remaining olive oil, chopped chile, and lemon zest. Stir in the sauce.

7   Divide the spaghetti among warmed bowls and top with the mussels and sauce. Serve immediately.

	for 2	for 6	for 20	for 50
mussels, debearded and scrubbed	1 lb/450 g	3 lb/1.4 kg	11 lb/5 kg	–
extra virgin olive oil	2 tbsp	6 tbsp	1¼ cups/300 ml	–
garlic cloves, crushed	1 small	2	4	–
fresh parsley, chopped	2 tbsp	½ cup/30 g	1⅔ cups/100 g	–
white wine	2 tbsp	6 tbsp	1 cup/250 ml	–
cherry tomatoes (preferably Pachino), quartered	⅓ cup/50 g	⅔ cup/100 g	1¾ cups/250 g	–
fresh spaghetti	12 oz/350 g	2¼ lb/1 kg	6½ lb/3 kg	–
red chile, seeded and finely chopped	½	2	2	–
zest from organic lemon	¼	½	1	–
salt	to taste	to taste	to taste	–

Rabbit alla Cacciatora

1   Put the olive oil into a Dutch oven or casserole dish and heat over medium-low heat. Stir in the onions, red and yellow bell peppers, and cook until softened.

2   Stir in the garlic and continue to cook over low heat until golden.

3   Add the wine and boil until reduced by half.

4   Season the rabbit portions with salt and black pepper, then place in the pot. Add the tomatoes, broth (stock), and herbs.

5   Cover and cook on the stove for 5 hours or until the rabbit is falling off the bone. Remove the herb stems from the Dutch oven.

6   If the sauce is too thin, remove the rabbit pieces and keep warm, then boil the sauce to thicken it to the desired consistency. Taste and season as required.

7   Add the capers and serve with unsalted sourdough bread.

	for 2	for 6	for 20	for 50
extra virgin olive oil	1 tbsp	1 tbsp	3 tbsp	–
yellow onions, finely chopped	¾ cup/120 g	2 cups/350 g	5½ cups/900 g	–
red bell peppers, finely chopped	1	2	7	–
yellow bell peppers, finely chopped	1	2	7	–
garlic cloves, minced, finely chopped	1	2 small	7	–
white wine	2 tbsp	6 tbsp	1 cup/250 ml	–
tomatoes, peeled, seeded, and finely diced	4 tbsp	scant ½ cup/85 g	1½ cups/250 g	–
rabbits, portioned, organs (offal) retained	1	3	9	–
chicken broth (stock)	3 cups/750 ml	9 cups/2.3 L	7½ qt/7 L	–
fresh thyme sprigs	2	6	18	–
fresh rosemary sprigs	1	2	7	–
sprigs of fresh marjoram	1	2	7	–
unsalted capers	1 tbsp	3 tbsp	⅔ cup/150g	–
salt and black pepper	to taste	to taste	to taste	–
unsalted sourdough bread slices, to serve	4	12	40	–

Tiramisu

1 For the savoiardi (sponge fingers), preheat the oven to 375°F/180°C/gas mark 5.

2 Line a baking sheet with parchment paper.

3 Beat the egg yolks and sugar with an electric mixer until pale and thick and the mixture trails a ribbon from the beaters. Gradually beat in the flour.

4 Beat the egg whites until increased in volume and just holding their shape, then carefully fold into the egg yolk mixture. (If using the same beaters, clean thoroughly before whisking the whites.)

5 Transfer the mixture to a pastry (piping) bag with a ½-inch (1-cm) plain tip (nozzle). Pipe the mixture into 3-inch (7.5-cm) lengths onto the parchment paper.

6 Bake in the center of the oven for 10–12 minutes or until golden and set.

7 Place on a wire rack to cool completely.

8 To make the mascarpone custard filling, beat the egg yolks and the sugar with an electric mixer until pale and thick.

9 Stir in the mascarpone cheese.

10 Whisk the egg whites until just stiff and fold into the mascarpone mixture.

11 To assemble, place the espresso in a shallow bowl and stir in the sugar to dissolve.

12 Dip half the savoiardi into the espresso and use to line the bottom of a serving dish.

13 Top with half of the mascarpone custard.

14 Repeat with the remaining savoiardi and mascarpone custard.

15 Sift the unsweetened cocoa powder over the top to finish. Refrigerate for at least 4 hours or overnight before serving.

for the savoardi (sponge fingers)	for 2	for 6	for 20	for 50
eggs, separated	–	2	7	11
superfine (caster) sugar	–	⅓ cup/65 g	1 cup/200 g	2½ cups/500 g
all-purpose (plain) flour	–	½ cup/65 g	1⅔ cups/200 g	4 cups/500 g

for the mascarpone filling	for 2	for 6	for 20	for 50
eggs, separated	–	2	6	14
superfine (caster) sugar	–	½ cup/50 g	¾ cup/150 g	1½ cups/350 g
mascarpone cheese	–	scant 1 cup/200 g	2½ cups/600 g	5½ cups/1.3 kg

to assemble	for 2	for 6	for 20	for 50
espresso	–	scant ½ cup/100 ml	1¼ cups/300 ml	2¾ cups/675 ml
superfine (caster) sugar	–	2 tsp	2½ tbsp	5½ tbsp
unsweetened cocoa powder	–	½ tsp	2 tsp	1½ tbsp

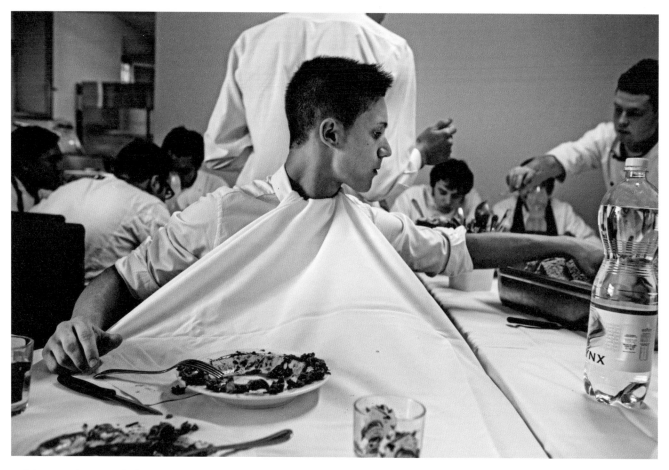

← Salmon teriyaki is a popular favorite among the team (p. 209).

← Seeing double with twins Andrea (left) and Luca (right) Garelli (previous pages).

↑ A waiter keeps his shirt clean for service.

→ *Tagliatelle con il ragù di bollito;* "Ragù is life," says Andrea Garelli, cellar manager.

Pierre Gagnaire

Location
Paris, France

Established
1996

Head chef
Pierre Gagnaire

Executive chef
Michel Nave

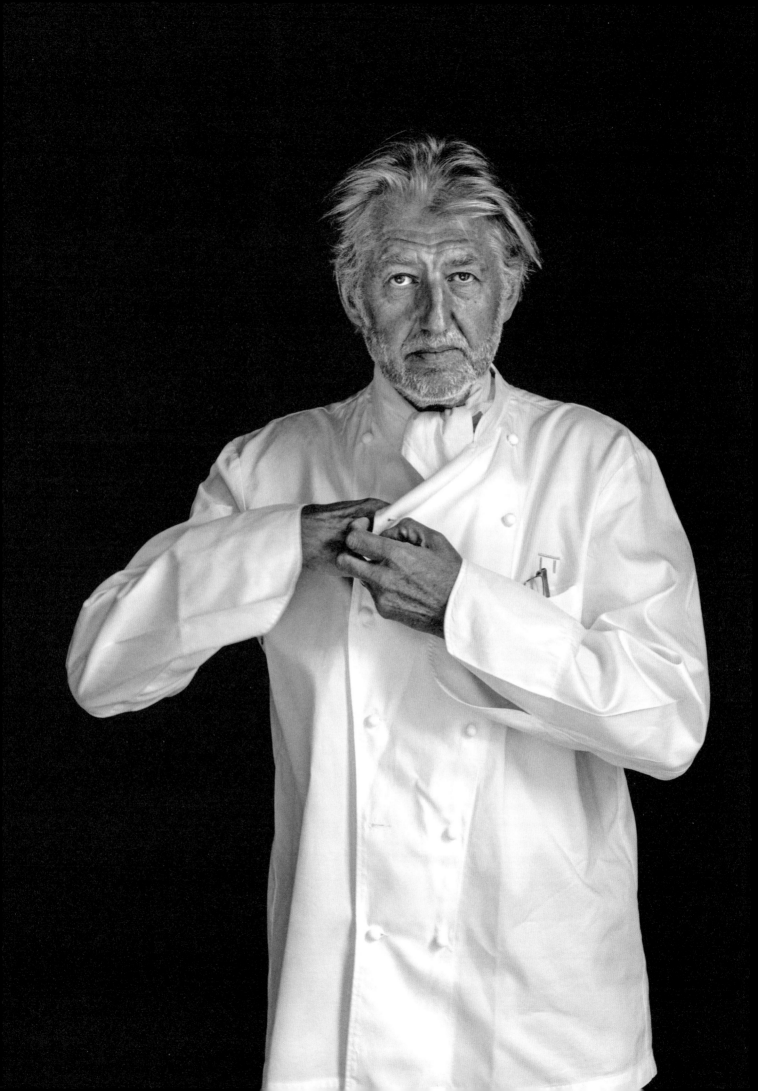

← Protective carpets safeguard the dining room
before service (previous pages).

← ↑ Chefs readying themselves for the staff meal
(left and top).

→   Pierre Gagnaire embossed copper pans
(overleaf).

Pierre Gagnaire

Pierre Gagnaire

Pierre Gagnaire is a Parisian icon, the very essence of Frenchness. The restaurant's techniques and attention to detail are impeccable, and when you see the staff meal being prepared it's like holding up a mirror to the sort of effort that goes into the dining room.

If the restaurant is French haute cuisine, the staff meal is all about French home cooking. It's often something very classic such as a spring vegetable soup, pâté and a juicy roast chicken, always written up on a special staff meal menu. But the names of the dishes reveal that it's also very driven by regional specialities. In other places you would just get melon soup or roast potatoes, for example, but here it's *soupe d'été* and *pommes alexia*. It shows respect to present a regional speciality in that way, to pick the appellation and then demonstrate very precisely how the dish should be done.

It suits a restaurant so deeply rooted in French cooking, and Pierre is very good at nurturing highly talented chefs with exacting standards. Staff meals are no different. They are planned two weeks in advance, and a schedule of what the staff are going to eat, and when, is then put up on the wall. It may not have the intimacy of sitting down and eating together, but it feels incredibly authentic. "If the staff meal is good, everybody is smiling. It's like good weather," says Sidney Redel, second de cuisine, who is in charge of it.

Chefs here work long hours and never sit down; front of house load their food onto what look like airline meal trays and take them down to a seriously utilitarian dining room in the basement, and the maître'd and sommelier set a little table for themselves in the dining room. Yet the food is always cooked with pride and precision: proper French home cooking with vegetables and salads, soups, meat, and on Saturdays and Sundays desserts—leftovers from the week that would otherwise be thrown away.

"When I sign up to do a new restaurant, I do it not only for me but for my team," Pierre says. "I am a celebrity in the street, but in the restaurant I am a part of what we do." He allows for a bit of playfulness—evidenced by the fact that the team are so happy and united—but not for one moment do you forget that this is a deeply serious, staunchly French restaurant. It is something they can all be proud of, but it is also something they work hard to protect.

Summer Soup

→ p. 228

1   Put all the ingredients in a nonreactive bowl and place in the refrigerator for 1 hour.

2   Puree the ingredients in a blender or food processor, then pass through a strainer (sieve) to remove the seeds and tomato skin.

3   Freeze the puree in an ice cream maker according to the manufacturer's directions. Transfer to a freezer container until required. Let soften for 10 minutes before serving.

	for 2	for 6	for 20	for 50
watermelon, peeled and cut into cubes	½ cup/75 g	1½ cups/225 g	4½ cups/675 g	–
ogen or cantaloupe melon, peeled and cubed	⅓ cup/40 g	¾ cup/120 g	2⅓ cups/350 g	–
red currants, stems removed	¼ cup/25 g	⅔ cup/75 g	2 cups/225 g	–
tomatoes, finely chopped	⅔ cup/100 g	1¾ cups/300 g	5⅓ cups/900 g	–
raspberries	¼ cup/35 g	¾ cup/100 g	2½ cups/300 g	–

Pommes Alexia

→ p. 225

1   Preheat the oven to 350°F/180°C/gas mark 4.

2   Pierce the potatoes several times with a sharp knife so
    that they will not explode in the oven. Rub them with salt,
    then place in the center of the oven and bake for about
    40 minutes.

3   Cut the warm potatoes in half lengthwise and scoop out
    the insides. Push the warm potato through a potato ricer
    or strainer (sieve).

4   Stir in the olives and herbs, then season to taste
    with salt and black pepper. Divide into the number
    of portions required.

5   Soak the spring roll wrappers (rice sheets) in warm water
    to soften, then wrap the potato mixture into each of them.

6   Cook in a steam oven set to 80°C/200°F or in a steamer
    for about 10 minutes.

	for 2	for 6	for 20	for 50
large, floury potatoes	1	3	10	25
chopped black olives	3 tbsp	½ cup/50 g	1½ cups/150 g	4½ cups/450 g
fresh parsley, finely chopped	1 tbsp	3 tbsp	½ cup/30 g	1½ cups/75 g
fresh chives, finely chopped	1 tbsp	3 tbsp	½ cup/30 g	1½ cups/75 g
rice spring roll wrappers (rice sheets)	2	6	20	50
salt and black pepper	to taste	to taste	to taste	to taste

Chicken Jean Vignard

→ p. 225

1   Preheat the oven to 350°F/180°C/gas mark 4.

2   Remove and discard the skin from the chicken, if desired.

3   Heat the oil in a skillet or frying pan over medium heat. Season the chicken with salt, then brown the chicken pieces on all sides. Place in an ovenproof dish in a single layer.

4   Add the onions to the pan and cook over medium-low heat until just starting to brown. Add the garlic and cook for another 2 minutes.

5   Add the white wine to the hot pan to deglaze, scraping any browned sediment from the bottom.

6   Stir in the tomato paste (puree), thyme, and bay leaves. Cook, stirring, for a couple of minutes until it darkens slightly in color. Stir in the mustard.

7   Spread the sauce over the chicken pieces, cover with foil, and bake in the oven for 1½ hours or until cooked through. Stir the cream through the sauce, adjust the seasoning, and serve immediately.

	for 2	for 6	for 20	for 50
free-range chicken breasts	2	6	20	50
(or free-range chicken thighs, if using)	4	12	40	100
oil, for frying	1 tbsp	4 tbsp	¾ cup/175 ml	1¾ cups/400 ml
onions, finely chopped	1 small	1 large	4½ cups/750 g	8 cups/1.8 kg
cloves garlic	1	3	10	25
white wine	1 tbsp	3 tbsp	¾ cup/175 ml	1⅔ cups/400 ml
tomato paste (puree)	3 tbsp	⅔ cup/150 ml	2 cups/500 ml	5 cups/1.2 L
sprigs fresh thyme	2	6	20	50
bay leaves	¼	½	2	5
Dijon mustard	5 tbsp	scant 1 cup/200 ml	3 cups/700 ml	7½ cups/1.8 L
heavy (double) cream	2 tbsp	6 tbsp	1¼ cups/300 ml	3 cups/750 ml
salt	to taste	to taste	to taste	to taste

← Raising a glass in the staff dining room at
Pierre Gagnaire (previous pages).

↑ Summer Soup (p. 222) provides the appetizer
in this staff meal.

↑ Taking a break from the kitchen.

Quay

Location
Sydney, Australia

Established
1998

Head chef
Peter Gilmore

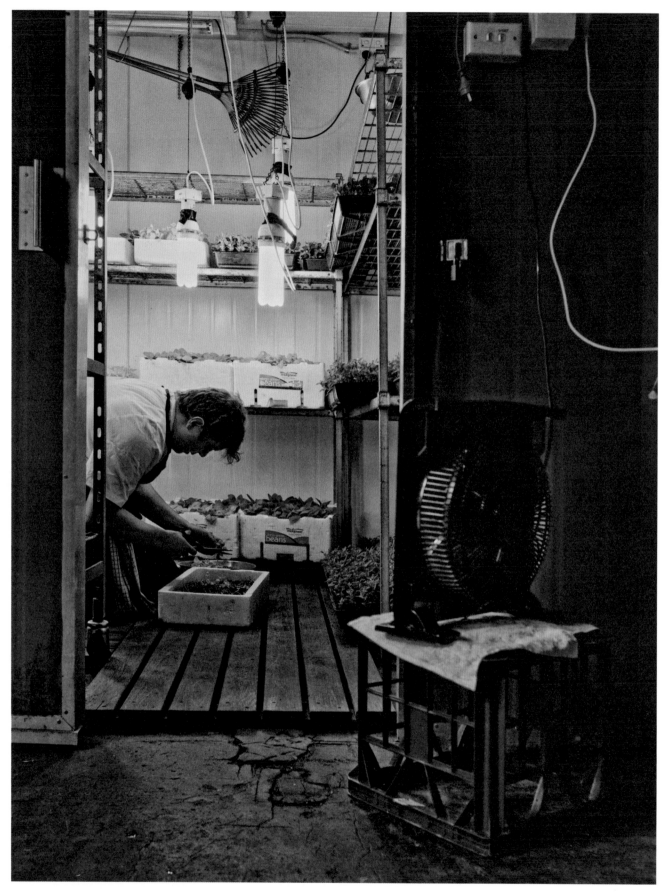

← From left to right: Mark Firla, Tuan Nguyen, Richard Ousby, and Kasper Christensen enjoy a break at one of the world's most iconic views for lunch (previous pages).

↑ → Making the most of limited space, a growing room is squirreled away across the road from the restaurant in the Quay offices.

Quay

Quay is a paradox. On the one hand, it has a fantastic glassed-in dining room with one of the best views in the world—it's sandwiched on the docks between the harbor bridge and the opera house—on the other, a kitchen with a low ceiling and no windows at all.

On top of that, the first question anyone asks when booking a table is: "Is there a cruise liner in the dock?" Monster ships regularly drop anchor right outside the dining room, blocking the view. Working conditions can be a little trying, and yet Quay is widely agreed to be among the best restaurants in Australia with some of the happiest staff in the world. It's a glass half-full kind of place, thanks largely to head chef Peter Gilmore's infectiously positive attitude—and they turn out amazing food to boot.

Think of it as fusion done really well. The kitchen has a passion for Asian influences, local farm-grown products, and seafood, and they come together in ways that are incredibly expressive, delicately presented yet explosively flavored. The staff meal is similarly based on big, explosive flavors, and each station has a shelf where leftovers and scraps are stashed to go into it. That's where the fun begins.

"My favorite thing is to do treats for the staff," says sous chef Analiese Gregory, who is in charge of planning the staff meal, and she's deeply aware that these kinds of gesture can make all the difference. The staff meal is as playful and well conceived as anything that goes out to the dining room, if simpler in content. Kitchen members are encouraged to cook dishes from their various national backgrounds, which keeps the meal interesting and varied as well as giving junior staff an opportunity to showcase their own talents. It's all about morale-boosting, crowd-satisfying, taste bud-dazzling dishes such as Chinese-style steamed buns, salt-and-pepper squid, devilishly hot Thai green curries, and Lamingtons—a quintessentially Australian sponge cake filled with cream and rolled in coconut. In essence, it's the kind of generous food that's guaranteed to raise a smile.

Along the way the team have become masters of making the most of what they've got, and they are surrounded by one of the most extraordinary harbors on earth. If the sun is shining, they take their plates outside to the terrace, fashioning a makeshift dining table and chairs out of upturned crates. If it pours with rain—and it often does—they head upstairs to a private function room, where there's a couch, kick off their shoes, and just flop.

The result is a fine dining restaurant that is laid-back and joyous, one that oozes good vibes.

Salt-and-Pepper Squid

→ p. 240

1 Make the spice mix by combining all the ground spices and salt.

2 Fry the chiles and scallions (spring onions) in a little oil and set aside.

3 Mix the club soda (soda water), all-purpose (plain) flour, and baking powder to make a batter.

4 Coat the squid trimmings in the batter and let drain slightly for a couple of minutes.

5 Combine the potato flour and cornstarch (cornflour) and coat the battered squid with it. Shake off the extra flour.

6 Heat the oil in a large saucepan and fry the squid in a couple of batches in the hot oil.

7 Coat the hot squid with the spice mix and toss through the chile and scallions.

8 Serve immediately.

for the spice mix	for 2	for 6	for 20	for 50
ground celery seeds	¼ tsp	½ tsp	1 tsp	–
ground long pepper	¼ tsp	½ tsp	1 tsp	–
ground black pepper	½ tsp	1½ tsp	1 tbsp	–
ground Sichuan pepper	½ tsp	2 tsp	4 tsp	–
ground Chinese five spice	½ tsp	2 tsp	4 tsp	–
sea salt	1 tbsp	3 tbsp	6 tbsp	–

for the squid				
long red chiles, finely sliced	1	2	6	–
scallions (spring onions) white part only, finely sliced	½ bunch	1½ bunches	4 bunches	–
club soda (soda water)	5 tbsp	scant 1 cup/200 ml	2½ cups/600 ml	–
all purpose (plain) flour	2 tbsp	⅔ cup/75 g	1⅔ cups/200 g	–
baking powder	pinch	½ tsp	1½ tsp	–
squid trimmings	7 oz/200 g	1¼ lb/600 g	4½ lb/2 kg	–
potato flour	⅔ cup/75 g	1¾ cups/200 g	5¼ cups/600 g	–
cornstarch (cornflour)	3 tbsp	⅔ cup/75 g	1⅔ cups/200 g	–
canola or vegetable oil	8½ cups/2 L	12½ cups/3 L	20 cups/5 L	–

Quay's Green Chicken Curry

1   Preheat the oven to 350°F/180°C/gas mark 4.

2   Place all of the ingredients for the curry paste into a food processor and process thoroughly until you have a smooth paste.

3   In a large ovenproof pan, heat the grapeseed oil. Sauté the curry paste in the oil, stirring constantly, until fragrant. Add half of the coconut cream and cook over medium heat until reduced and the coconut cream has split.

4   Add the chicken broth (stock) and return to a low simmer.

5   Meanwhile, heat a skillet or frying pan and seal the chicken legs in batches.

6   Add the chicken legs to the pan with the curry sauce, making sure that they are completely submerged in the sauce. Cover the pan with foil, transfer to the preheated oven, and cook for 45 minutes.

7   Take the pan from the oven and remove the chicken legs from the sauce. Set the chicken legs aside, keeping them warm. Return the pan to the stove and reduce the sauce over high heat until it thickens.

8   Add the sugar, fish sauce, lime juice, and remaining coconut cream to the pan and stir to combine. Bring the sauce back to a boil and return the chicken legs to the pan. Stir in the kaffir lime leaves and cilantro (coriander) leaves and serve immediately with coconut rice.

for the curry paste	for 2	for 6	for 20	for 50
medium-hot green chiles, finely chopped with seeds	–	½ cup/75 g	1⅓ cups/200 g	3⅓ cups/500 g
kaffir lime zest	–	1	4	10
garlic, chopped	–	4 tbsp	½ cup/75 g	1½ cups/200 g
lemongrass, finely sliced	–	¾ cup/50 g	2¼ cups/150 g	6 cups/400 g
cilantro (coriander) stems and leaves	–	1¾ cups/75 g	5 cups/200 g	1 lb 2oz/500 g
tumeric root, peeled and chopped	–	2½ tbsp	⅓ cup/40g	1 cup/100 g
onion, chopped	–	¾ cup/125 g	2 cups/320 g	5 cups/800 g
fresh ginger, peeled and chopped	–	2½ tbsp	⅓ cup/40 g	1 cup/300 g
galangal, peeled and chopped	–	1 tbsp	2½ tbsp	6 tbsp
roasted shrimp paste	–	1 tbsp	3 tbsp	½ cup/100 g
coriander seeds, lightly roasted and ground	–	3 tbsp	½ cup/40 g	1¼ cups/100 g
cumin seeds, lightly roasted and ground	–	2 tbsp	5 tbsp	1 cup/100 g
grapeseed oil	–	5 tbsp	⅔ cup/150 ml	1 ½ cups/350 ml
salt	–	large pinch	1 tbsp	2¾ tbsp

for the curry				
coconut cream	–	scant 1 cup/200 ml	3⅓ cups/800 ml	8½ cups/2 L
chicken broth (stock)	–	3⅓ cups/800 ml	8½ cups/2 L	20 cups/5 L
chicken legs	–	6	20	50
brown sugar or jaggery, packed	–	1 tbsp	4 tbsp	⅔ cup/150 g
Thai fish sauce	–	1 tbsp	3 tbsp	scant ½ cup/100 ml
lime juice	–	2 tbsp	5 tbsp	scant 1 cup/200 ml
kaffir lime leaves, julienned at the last minute	–	5	12	30
cilantro (coriander) leaves, chopped	–	½ small bunch	1 large bunch	3 bunches
coconut rice	–	to serve	to serve	to serve

Coconut and Cherry Lamingtons

→ p. 243

Make the sponge and filling
one day before icing.

1   To make the sponge, preheat the oven to 350°F/180°C/
    gas mark 4.

2   Prepare a half-sheet pan or roasting pan by lining it with
    parchment paper.

3   Put the eggs and sugar in a large stand mixer and beat until
    thick, pale, and doubled in volume.

4   Sift the flour and fold through the egg mixture in 2–3
    batches. Turn into the prepared pan. The mixture should
    be 2 inches (5 cm) thick.

5   Bake in the center of the oven for about 35 minutes or until
    set and golden brown.

6   Remove from the oven and let cool on a wire rack.
    Wrap in plastic wrap (clingfilm) and store at room
    temperature overnight.

7   To make the filling, mix the sugar, milk and cream together.
    Bring to a boil, then whisk in the coconut milk powder. Let
    cool, then refrigerate overnight.

8   Before using, whisk and then add the heavy (double) cream
    and whisk until soft peaks form.

9   To make the chocolate glaze, sift together the confectioners'
    (icing) sugar and cocoa powder. Whisk in the corn or glucose
    syrup, milk and water.

10 Bring to a boil, then pass through a strainer (sieve). While it
    is still warm add the gelatin sheets. Whisk well and let cool
    to room temperature.

11 To assemble, cut the sponge into 20 squares and cut each
    in half horizontally. Layer the coconut cream and cherry jam
    in the center.

12 Pour the chocolate glaze over the tops and sides of the cakes
    and sprinkle on the grated coconut.

for the sponge	for 2	for 6	for 20	for 50
eggs, beaten	–	–	10	–
superfine (caster) sugar	–	–	1½ cups/300 g	–
all-purpose (plain) flour	–	–	2 cups/250 g	–
for the coconut cream filling				
superfine (caster) sugar	–	–	¾ cup/150 g	–
milk	–	–	1¼ cups/300 ml	–
light (single) cream	–	–	1¼ cups/300 ml	–
coconut milk powder	–	–	2¾ cups/300 g	–
heavy (double) cream	–	–	2 cups/500 ml	–
cherry preserves or jam	–	–	⅔ cup/200 g	–
for the chocolate glaze				
confectioners' (icing) sugar	–	–	8 cups/1 kg	–
unsweetened cocoa powder	–	–	2 cups/170 g	–
corn syrup or glucose syrup	–	–	⅓ cup/100 g	–
milk	–	–	1 cup/250 ml	–
water	–	–	1 cup/250 ml	–
gelatin sheets	–	–	2	–
grated, sweetened coconut	–	–	1½ cups/100 g	–

← Salt-and-Pepper Squid (p. 238).

↑ → Key ingredients to happiness: morale-boosting, crowd-satisfying, taste bud-dazzling dishes (Coconut and Cherry Lamingtons, p. 240).

→ The family meal is eaten standing up in Quay's busy kitchen (overleaf).

Roberta's

Carlo Mirarchi

Location
New York City, USA

Established
2008

Head chef
Carlo Mirarchi

← Produce delivery on the back streets of Brooklyn.

↑ Oliver Vonderahe—volunteer woodcutter and occasional pizza maker—sorts oak, cherry, maple, and hickory wood sourced from Pennsylvania for Roberta's cultish pizzas.

→ David Rosenfeld (overleaf).

Roberta's

Roberta's is a quiet success story that came out of nowhere. An obscure yard in Brooklyn is a highly unlikely place to stumble across one of New York City's best restaurants, but something about it just worked.

Chef Carlo Mirarchi is very shy, but takes a hugely free-spirited approach to the way he runs the business. Roberta's was named after his partner's mother (he named the more recently opened Blanca after his own), and it's as much a homage to family—in the extended sense—as it is to food. Such is the allure of the place that since opening in 2008, the team has grown to somewhere between seventy and ninety people, depending on who's there on any given day. Many simply hang around doing odd jobs—like the woodcutter who also delivers bread in the morning on his bike—others are actors, musicians, writers or artists moonlighting as waiters or kitchen staff. There's no doubt that everyone loves being here, and so they have a motto: feed people who work hard.

"We let people do what they are good at." Carlo says. "We are not into micro-managing. We try to set them up to succeed and do things the way they want to do them. The most important thing for us is to find the right people and put them in the right places. We are not searching for talent so much as simply letting them grow."

Three kitchens take turns to cook the staff meal on different days. So it tends to be created out of a "walkabout," picking up leftovers from the different stations, and is nearly always something people can carry around with them. Cook Aaron "Knuckles" describes it as "brainstorming with everything," and everyone has their special. His is boiled pork and beans stuffed into a focaccia. Melissa Weller, the head baker, makes fresh bagels in experimental flavors that can't be served in the restaurant, and David Rosenfeld, sous chef at Blanca, offers chopped chicken livers, homemade cream cheese, or egg mayonnaise. If there isn't enough food to go around, which easily happens in a restaurant that opens at 8 a.m. and serves nonstop until the last person has gone home, there is always the to-die-for Pizza Margherita.

Then the team scatter through the various kitchens, the bakery, and the yard, nearly always ending up congregated around the wood-fired bread oven, where they talk about the important stuff: friends, family, food, and life. It feels more like a foodie commune than the revered pizza joint-cum-Michelin-starred restaurant that it is; but above all, it feels remarkably free.

"If you open up a restaurant and your only goal is to get three Michelin stars, then I wonder who are you cooking for," Carlo says. "It defeats its purpose. I never want to work that way."

Roberta's Bagels

→ p. 252

1 Sift the flour into the bowl of a stand mixer. Make a well in the center and add the remaining ingredients except for the baking soda (bicarbonate of soda). If fresh yeast is not available substitute active dry (easy-blend dried) yeast, using 2¼ teaspoons dry yeast for ⅔ oz/187 g fresh yeast. If you do not have natural leaven double the amount of yeast called for and substitute plain (natural) yogurt with live cultures for the leaven.

2 Using the dough hook, mix together on the first speed for 3 minutes, then on the second speed for 5 minutes. Cover the dough with oiled plastic wrap (clingfilm) and let stand at room temperature for 1 hour.

3 Knead the dough lightly for 10 seconds, then divide into equal sized pieces. Roll each piece into a long rope about 8 inches (20 cm) long. Bring the ends together and overlap them by about 1½ inches (4 cm) to make a ring. With several fingers placed on the seam going through the center of the ring, roll the dough back and forth on the counter (work surface) to join the ends together. Exaggerate the size of the bagel hole because it will shrink as the bagel rises.

4 Line a large baking sheet with parchment paper. Dust the parchment with flour. Place each shaped bagel on the parchment about 2 inches (5 cm) apart. Cover with oiled plastic wrap (clingfilm) and refrigerate overnight. At the bakery, the bagels rest for about 20 hours.

5 The next day, preheat the oven to 350°F/180°C/gas mark 4.

6 Fill a large saucepan with water and bring to a boil. Add the baking soda.

7 Drop the bagels one at a time into the water. After about 30 seconds, remove the bagels from the water, using a slotted spatula, and place on a parchment-lined baking sheet. The bagels should float to the top during poaching, indicating that they are properly risen (proved).

8 Bake the bagels in the oven for 20–25 minutes or until golden brown. Remove to a wire rack and cool for 5 minutes, then peel the bagels from the parchment paper. Return to the rack to cool.

	for 2	for 6	for 20	for 50
high-protein (strong) bread flour	–	2 cups/300 g	7⅓ cups/1 kg	5½ lb/2.5 kg
barley malt syrup	–	1 tbsp	2½ tbsp	⅓ cup/125 g
granulated sugar	–	1 tbsp	4 tbsp	⅔ cup/125 g
sea salt	–	2 tsp	2 tbsp	5 tbsp + 1 tsp
fresh yeast	–	½ tsp	1 tsp	2½ tsp
natural leaven	–	5 tbsp	1 cup/250 ml	2½ cups/600 ml
baking soda (bicarbonate of soda), for boiling	–	1 tsp	1 tsp	1 tsp

Bagel Toppings

→ p. 252

1 First make the cream cheese. Heat the milk and cream to 188°F/73°C, stir in the vinegar, remove from the heat, and let stand for 15 minutes off the heat.

2 Line a large strainer (sieve) or colander with cheesecloth (muslin). Remove the curds from the pan, using a slotted spoon, and put into the lined strainer (sieve). Let drain for 2 hours.

3 Puree the drained curds with the crème fraiche and season with lemon juice and salt to taste.

4 Prepare the chicken livers by removing any membranes, green coloring, and stringy parts.

5 Put enough oil into a large sauté pan to coat the bottom. Heat over medium-high heat. Season the livers generously with salt, then cook until golden brown on all sides. Remove the livers from the pan and set aside. Let cool.

6 Reduce the heat to medium-low and add the onions. Cook until browned, stirring occasionally. Let cool.

7 In the meantime, place the eggs in boiling water, reduce to a simmer, and cook for 10 minutes. Drain and cover with cold water. Crack the shells lightly to help with peeling.

8 Put the livers, onions, and eggs in a food processor and pulse until smooth.

9 For the egg salad, put the eggs into a large saucepan and cover with cold water. Put over medium heat and bring to a boil, increasing the heat, if necessary. Once boiling, reduce the heat to a simmer and time the eggs to cook for 8 minutes.

10 Drain the eggs as above. When cool, peel the eggs. Finely chop them, then mix in the mayonnaise and mustard. Season with salt and black pepper to taste.

for the cream cheese	for 2	for 6	for 20	for 50
whole (full-fat) milk	–	1½ cups/350 ml	5 cups/1.2 L	12½ cups/3 L
heavy (double) cream	–	½ cup/120 ml	1⅔ cups/400 ml	4¼ cups/1 L
white distilled vinegar	–	4 tbsp	¾ cup/175 ml	2 cups/500 ml
crème fraîche	–	1½ tbsp	5 tbsp	¾ cup/175 ml
lemon juice	–	to taste	to taste	to taste
salt	–	to taste	to taste	to taste

for the chicken livers				
chicken livers	–	12 oz/350 g	5 lb/2.2 kg	12½ lb/5.7 kg
sweet (Spanish) onions, minced (finely diced)	–	1 small	2 large	5 large
eggs	–	2	6	15
vegetable oil or spray				
salt	–	to taste	to taste	to taste

for the egg salad				
eggs	–	6	20	50
mayonnaise	–	3 tbsp	¾ cup/175 ml	2½ cups/600 ml
Dijon mustard	–	1 tbsp	2½ tbsp	6 tbsp
salt and black pepper	–	to taste	to taste	to taste

Roberta's Ribs and Green Beans

→ p. 257

1   Melt the pork fat (lard) in a large roasting pan large enough to hold the ribs. Brown the ribs in the fat. Remove the ribs from the pan and set aside.

2   Preheat the oven to 175°F/85°C/gas mark ¼.

3   Stir the onions into the fat and cook, stirring occasionally, until golden. Add the garlic and cook for a couple of minutes longer.

4   Add the Dr. Pepper to the hot pan to deglaze. Scrape any browned sediment from the bottom of the pan. Return the ribs to the pan.

5   Add the hot sauce and salt, then pour in enough water to cover the ribs.

6   Cover the roasting pan and place in the oven for 6 hours. Set aside to cool.

7   Remove the ribs from the roasting pan and place in a single layer on a rimmed baking sheet.

8   Boil the braising liquid until reduced to a syrupy consistency. Brush the ribs with the sauce, reserving some sauce for serving.

9   Preheat the oven to 450°F/250°C/gas mark 8.

10 Place the ribs in the hot oven for 5–10 minutes to brown and heat through. Serve hot with the extra sauce.

11 Trim and wash the beans, dry, and then place on a baking sheet and roast in the oven for 5 minutes at 480°F/250°C/gas mark 9.

12 Let them cool, then toss with the olive oil, balsamic vinegar, and sea salt.

for the ribs	for 2	for 6	for 20	for 50
pork fat (lard)	1 tbsp	4 tbsp	½ cup/120 g	1½ cups/300 g
pork ribs	2¼ lb/1 kg	4½ lb/2 kg	13 lb/6 kg	33 lb/15 kg
sweet (Spanish) onions, chopped	¾	1½	4	10
garlic, crushed	3 cloves	10 cloves	2 heads	5 heads
Dr. Pepper	1 cup/250 ml	3 cups/750 ml	8½ cups/2 L	6¼ qt/6 L
Frank's Red Hot Sauce (cayenne pepper sauce)	1 tsp	1 tbsp	3 tbsp	scant ½ cup/100 ml
salt	½ tsp	2 tsp	2½ tbsp	5 tbsp

for the beans				
green beans	–	1¾ lb/800 g	5¼ lb/2.4 kg	13 lb/6 kg
olive oil	–	3 tbsp	½ cup/120 ml	1¼ cups/300 ml
balsamic vinegar	–	1 tbsp	3 tbsp	scant ½ cup/100 ml
sea salt to taste	–	to taste	to taste	to taste

← Leftovers are clearly labeled to ensure nothing goes to waste.

↑ 12 Noon: Aaron "Knuckles" Buktus starts his daily sweep for leftovers.

→ Alice Allemano. "Emergency" pizza is fired up in a wood oven when leftovers fall short (following page).

Royal Mail

Location
Dunkeld, Australia

Established
2008

Head chef
Dan Hunter

Sous chefs
Jeff Trotter and Damien Neylon

← The Australian outback makes an ideal environment for the restaurant's organic gardens (previous pages).

↑ Gathering ingredients with Mount Sturgeon in the background (top).

↑ Feeding the chickens with kitchen scraps (above).

→ A legendary staff dish: Yenni's Fish-Head Curry (p. 271) uses a paste made from herbs and spices grown in the garden.

Royal Mail

There is a small, dusty town in the vast emptiness that is the state of Victoria, with one long, straight road running through it. In the middle of all that space is Royal Mail—ranked one of the best restaurants in Australia, but one that feels very far away from the rest of the world.

For the diner, this journey is rewarded with new flavors, such as the rare Monterey berry—the size of a grape, with great acidity and the aromas of pear, rose, and quince—and through them they see another side of Australia. But it also offers a unique opportunity for the people who work here. Sous chef Damien Neylon had long been a follower of Dan Hunter's food philosophy when he joined the team, attracted principally by access to the restaurant's 43,600 square feet (4,050 square meters) of organic gardens. "It's fantastic because nearly à hundred percent of the herbs, fruits, and vegetables we use are our own," he explains. "I love that things are not planted to become dishes, but that the dishes are created around what's available at the time. That's just as true for the staff meal. If you're using zucchini (courgette) for example, it might only be the flower in the restaurant, but in the staff meal the fruit is used in a myriad of different ways."

These days the staff meal at Royal Mail is very close to being vegetarian, often using protein like a flavoring or condiment as is typical of Thai and South East Asian food. One of the more legendary dishes is a fish-head curry, using a paste made from herbs and spices grown in the garden. It was the signature dish of Indonesian kitchen hand Yenni Montgomery, who has since sadly passed away, but the chefs continue to make her recipes and use them as part of their education. "I haven't traveled a lot," Damien says, "but I get to taste a little bit of everywhere at Royal Mail. You learn a lot from growing and eating those things, and seeing what other people do with them. In some ways it's the staff meal that has taught me how to cook, and that has really brought me forward as a chef."

When Dan took over the kitchen in 2007, he focused on promoting a deep belief that cooks need to be closely connected to their produce in order to bring a sense of terroir to the table. Cultural diversity is, of course, an enriching aspect of any kitchen, but Royal Mail has direct access to the produce to back it up. These days five members of the team spend several hours a day gardening and collecting fruit and vegetables for the restaurant, because this is seen as such an integral part of the kitchen. It gives a glimpse into a new level of Australian cuisine that goes far beyond farm to fork: one where produce and culinary influences are seamlessly integrated and chefs are deeply connected to the land.

Kingfish Wing Salad

→ p. 275

1   First make the smoked oil. Put the oil in a deep roasting pan. Place in the oven. Place the vine trimmings or wood chips in a second roasting pan and light.

2   Once the fire has burned out and the wood is "white" and still smoking, pour the oil over the embers and seal the smoke in with a lid. Let infuse for about 12 hours and store in glass jars or bottles.

3   To prepare the fish, preheat the oven to 400°F/200°C/ gas mark 6.

4   Put a ½-inch/1-cm thick layer of coarse sea (rock) salt in the bottom of a roasting pan. Put the fish skin side down in a single layer on the salt. Drizzle with olive oil and bake for 10–15 minutes.

5   Remove from the oven and let stand until cool enough to handle. Remove the skin and any membrane from the fish. Pull the fish into large flakes. Place the fish in a nonreactive container and cover with the smoked oil.

6   To make the salad, bring a large saucepan of seasoned water to a boil, add the eggs, and cook for 6 minutes, then refresh in seasoned ice water. Peel and cut into quarters.

7   Wash all of the salad greens (leaves) and herbs to remove any dirt. Dry in a salad spinner and reserve.

8   Segment the oranges and cut each segment in half, squeeze the juice from each segment, and mix with the moscatel vinegar, and olive oil, and seasoning. Retain the juiced orange segments.

9   Blanch the diced shallots briefly in hot water.

10 In a large bowl, dress the salad greens with the dressing and add the shallot, orange segments, cucumber and tomato. Toss to combine. Scatter with kingfish meat and soft boiled egg quarters.

for the smoked oil

extra virgin olive oil	–	–	2 cups/500 g	–
dry grape vine cuttings or wood chips	–	–	1 lb 2 oz/500 g	–

for the wings

	for 2	for 6	for 20	for 50
kingfish wings or fillets	2 x 6 oz/175 g	6 x 6 oz/175 g	20 x 6 oz/175 g	50 x 6 oz/175 g
sea (rock) salt	to cover	to cover	to cover	to cover
olive oil	to drizzle	to drizzle	to drizzle	to drizzle

for the salad

organic free-range eggs	2	6	20	50
lettuce leaves (Boston, bibb, baby gem, chicory)	4 cups/175 g	12 cups/500 g	3½ lb/1.7 kg	6¼ lb/2.8 kg
fresh herbs (chives, tarragon, fennel fronds)	1 tbsp	3 tbsp	⅔ cup/40 g	1½ cups/80 g
oranges, segmented, juice reserved	1	2	4	9
shallots, finely chopped	½	2	5	12
cucumbers, peeled and finely diced	¼	¾	2	5
assorted cherry tomatoes, halved or quartered	1 cup/140 g	3 cups/425 g	2½ lb/1.2 kg	7 lb/3 kg

for the dressing

juice from orange pulp (see above)				
aged moscatel vinegar	to taste	to taste	to taste	to taste
olive oil	to taste	to taste	to taste	to taste
salt and black pepper	to taste	to taste	to taste	to taste

Yenni's Fish-Head Curry

1 Coarsely chop all the ingredients for the spice paste except the sunflower oil, then grind in a spice grinder or pound with a mortar and pestle to a paste.

2 Put the sunflower oil in a large skillet or frying pan and heat over low heat. Add the spice paste and cook, stirring continuously, until fragrant and the oil separates from the paste.

3 Add the fish heads and cook until lightly browned. Add more oil, if necessary.

4 Add the coconut cream and season.

5 Peel the eggplants (aubergine) and dice into 1-inch/2-cm cubes.

6 Add the eggplants and simmer for about 2 hours or until the soup reduces slightly, the eggplants are tender, and the snapper heads have broken down.

7 Season with the fish sauce and lime juice.

8 Boil or steam the jasmine rice. Scatter over the fresh cilantro (coriander) leaves to serve.

for the spice paste	for 2	for 6	for 20	for 50
dried tamarind (assam) slices	–	½ oz/15 g	1½ oz/40 g	3¾ oz/100 g
whole candlenuts (Kemiri)	–	7	22	55
fresh turmeric	–	½ oz/15 g	1½ oz/40 g	3¾ oz/100 g
garlic cloves, peeled	–	3	10	25
shallots, coarsely chopped	–	3	10	25
granulated sugar	–	1 tsp	1 tbsp	2½ tbsp
ground coriander	–	1 tsp	1 tbsp	2½ tbsp
salt	–	1 tbsp	3 tbsp	7½ tbsp
Thai (bird's eye) chiles	–	1	4	10
mild red chiles	–	½	2	5
green chiles	–	½	2	5
bay leaves	–	2	6	15
stalks of lemongrass	–	½	2	5
kaffir lime leaves	–	3	10	25
for the curry				
sunflower oil	–	3 tbsp	6 tbsp	scant 1 cup/200 ml
Portland snapper heads	–	4½ lb/2 kg	13½ lb/6 kg	34 lb/15 kg
Thai fish sauce	–	to taste	to taste	to taste
Lebanese eggplants	–	2	10	25
coconut cream	–	2 cups/500 ml	6 cups/1.4 L	15 cups/3.5 L
fresh lime juice	–	to taste	to taste	to taste
to serve				
jasmine rice	–	1⅔ cups/300 g	5⅓ cups/1 kg	5½ lb/2.5 kg
fresh cilantro (coriander) leaves	–	4 tbsp	¾ cup/30 g	2 cups/80 g

Chocolate Ripple Cake

→ p. 273

1 Place the candy canes or peppermint crisp bars in the freezer and freeze for at least 3 hours. Remove from the freezer and smash into small pieces with a rolling pin. Set aside.

2 Halve the vanilla beans (pods) and remove the seeds.

3 Add the vanilla seeds to the cream and whisk to soft peaks using an electric mixer.

4 To assemble the cake, take a chocolate ripple cookie and, using a spatula (palette) knife, spread the back and front generously with the cream mixture. Take another cookie and repeat the process, using the cream to sandwich this cookie to the first.

5 Repeat until you have used all of the cookies and have a long row.

6 Take the remainder of the cream and spread over the top and sides of the row of cookies so they are no longer visible.

7 Sprinkle the smashed peppermint crisp bars over the cake. Refrigerate until 30 minutes before serving.

Ingredients	for 2	for 6	for 20	for 50
candy canes or Peppermint Crisp chocolate bars	–	2	6	15
vanilla beans (pods)	–	½	1	3
heavy (double) cream	–	1 cup/250 ml	3 cups/750 ml	7½ cups/1.8 L
Chocolate Ripple Cookies (thin chocolate biscuits)	–	6 oz/175 g	1¾ lb/800 g	4½ lb/2 kg

← 2:30 p.m.: lunch is served. From left to right: Tom Edwards, front right: Jeff Trotter, far right: Ermis Wilhelm (previous page).

← Damien Neylon.

↑ Clean up in the kitchen.

St. John

Location
London, UK

Established
1994

Chef owner
Fergus Henderson

Head chef
Chris Gillard

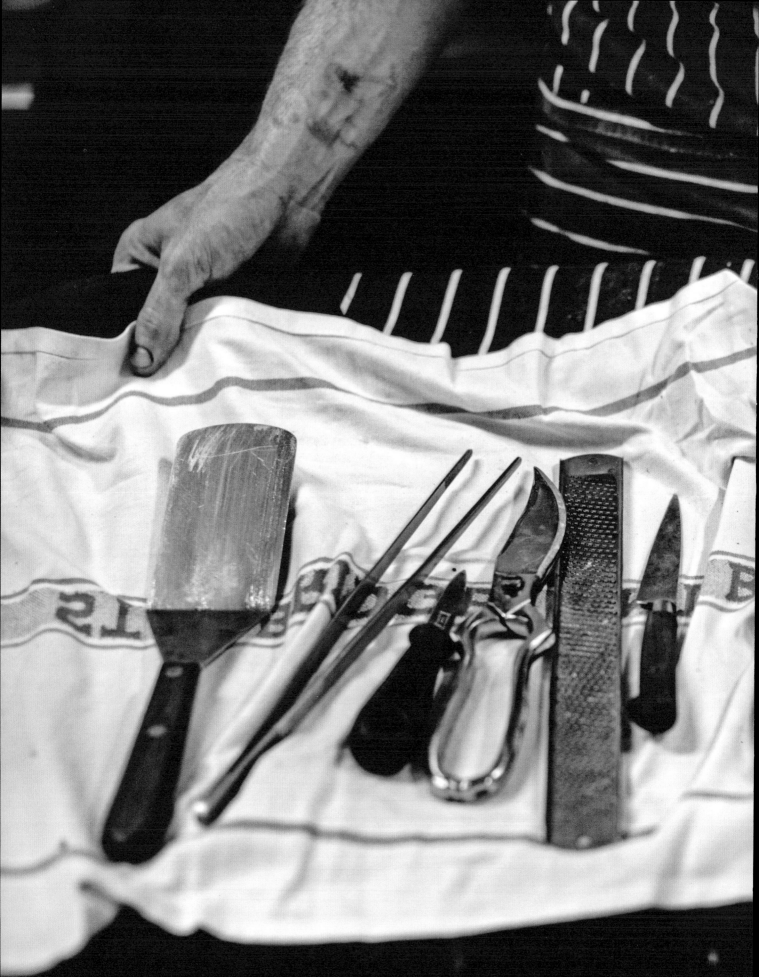

← Tools of the trade (previous page).

↑ 10 a.m.: preparing dining room for service.

→ Cut thinly the ox heart cooks quickly and evenly.

St. John

Is it possible to imagine a more quintessentially British restaurant than St. John? It's such a big part of the concept you can't escape it, and it fits perfectly with Fergus's belief in nose-to-tail eating. Located just around the corner from Smithfield, the biggest meat market in Britain, which dates back eight hundred years, St. John feels almost like a part of the neighborhood's history.

It's also one of the few places where the staff eat the same as the diners. The philosophy of using every part of the animal runs so deep that the staff have to be comfortable with it, to love it as much as Fergus. At St. John the cheaper cuts are viewed as the delicacy, and it's seen as a real perk of the job to eat this way. There is no fear of fat or organs (offal) or marrowbone—its all just pure passion for real food.

The staff meal, then, is regarded as such a vital part of the day that head chef Chris Gillard insists that no matter how busy they are, everyone sits down at the table at 11 a.m. and again at 5 p.m. to dig into some good, old-fashioned food. It might be deviled kidneys with mashed potatoes and gravy, thick-cut fries (chips) with slices of ox heart and homemade tartar sauce, or bread soaked in the cooking juices and rendered fat of a hunk of pork , washed down with a mug of tea or possibly a half pint of Guinness.

What gets everyone excited, though, is the Monday morning "big breakfast"—a classic British "fry-up" with all the trimmings. "It comes from that 'oh no, it's Monday' feeling, and takes the edge off a big weekend that probably started here on Friday," says sous chef Giles Edwards. "We all see it as treat, and psychologically that's a great way to start the week." It's become such an important part of the St. John culture that when a healthy Monday morning breakfast once appeared, involving fruit plates and oatmeal (porridge), there was mutiny in the ranks. It was never served again.

All this "togetherness" brings front of house and kitchen closer, and because the staff come from all over the world—particularly New Zealand and Australia—it's become a second home for a lot of people. They even hang out here on their days off. Even so, Giles remains pragmatic. "Nobody has ever called it 'family meal.' We find that a bit eerie, like you're trying to force the issue. And we don't go in for jargon or hierarchy either. We don't say 'chef,' we just use each other's names".

There is something very reassuring about this lack of pretension and the sight of the team gathered around a big table, competing over a newspaper crossword, gossiping, or planning a night out. They may come from all over the world, but they capture the essence of no-nonsense Britishness and that is exactly what you experience in the dining room.

St. John Big Breakfast

1 Heat the oven to 375°F/180°C/gas mark 5.

2 Put a thin coating of oil in a lipped baking sheet and heat on the stove over medium heat. Add the sausages and when starting to sizzle, put in the oven.

3 When done, place in a serving dish, cover with foil, and keep warm.

4 In a separate lipped baking sheet with a thin coating of oil, place the mushrooms flat side down. Dot each mushroom with some butter. Put in the oven with the sausages. Cook until the mushrooms are tender when pierced with a knife, remove from the oven, and keep warm.

5 Heat the broiler (grill). Put the bacon slices in a single layer on a baking sheet and broil (grill) on one side until brown. Turn the bacon over and broil on the other side until crisp. Keep warm.

6 Slice the blood sausage (black pudding) into ¼-inch (½-cm) slices. Heat a skillet or frying pan with a little oil over medium-high heat and fry the slices on each side to warm through and brown.

7 Put the baked beans into a saucepan over medium-low heat and warm through.

8 Put the eggs into the top part of a double boiler. Season with salt and black pepper. Beat with a fork until combined then whisk in the milk. Cook over simmering water, scraping the sides, until the eggs start to scramble. Add the remaining butter and fold in. Try to catch the moment when the eggs are soft and just cooked and before they become rubbery. Turn into a warmed serving dish and keep warm.

9 Toast the bread and serve.

	for 2	for 6	for 20	for 50
vegetable oil	for brushing	for brushing	for brushing	for brushing
Cumberland sausage or other good quality sausage	2	6	20	50
small Portabello mushrooms	2	6	20	50
butter	1 tbsp	2 tbsp/25 g	1 stick/¼ lb/120 g	2 sticks/½ lb/225 g
slices of bacon (streaky bacon)	4 oz/120 g	12 oz/375 g	2½ lb/1.25 kg	6½ lb/3 kg
blood sausage (black pudding)	2 slices	6 slices	1 ring	2 rings
15-oz (450-g) can baked beans	½ can	1½ cans	5 cans	12 cans
eggs	3	8	2 dozen	60 eggs
whole (full-fat) milk	2 tbsp	5 tbsp	1 cup/250 ml	2 cups/500 ml
bread for toast	4 slices	12 slices	40 slices	100 slices
salt and black pepper	to taste	to taste	to taste	to taste

to serve

steak (HP) sauce	to taste	to taste	to taste	to taste
ketchup	to taste	to taste	to taste	to taste

Deviled Kidneys

← p. 284

1   For the mashed potatoes, peel the potatoes and cut into even 1½-inch (3-cm) pieces. Put in a large saucepan and cover with cold water. Season with salt, then cover and bring to a boil. Turn the heat down to a simmer. Place the lid slightly ajar, then cook until the potatoes are tender when pierced with a knife. Drain in a colander, then return the hot potatoes to the warm pan to steam dry.

2   Put the butter in the pan with the potatoes. Put the milk in a saucepan and heat until it is steaming. Mash the potatoes with a potato masher or push though a ricer. Gradually stir in the hot milk until the desired consistency is reached. Season with salt. Do not overseason because it needs to serve as a foil for the strong flavors of the kidneys. Keep warm.

3   Cut the kidneys in half lengthwise to produce two equal halves. Peel away any membrane. Cut the white core out of the middle of the kidneys, using sharp, pointy scissors.

4   Put the flour, mustard powder, and ground cayenne in a large plastic bag. Season the kidneys with salt and black pepper, then place a handful of kidneys in the plastic bag. Shake well to coat them with the flour and spices. Remove the kidneys from the bag, shaking them as you work to remove any excess flour. Place them on a plate in a single layer.

5   It is important that the kidneys are cooked in a skillet or frying pan in a single layer, so you might need to cook the kidneys in batches, depending how many you are cooking and the size of your pan.

6   Heat three-quarters of the butter in a heavy skillet or frying pan over medium-high heat. When the bubbling stops and the butter starts to brown, add enough kidneys to fit in a single layer with a little space between them. Brown the kidneys evenly on both sides, then add the Worcestershire sauce.

7   Let the sauce bubble slightly, then add the chicken broth (stock) and simmer to thicken. When the kidneys feel firm, remove them with a slotted spoon to a warm dish and keep warm. If necessary, boil the sauce more until syrupy, then whisk in the remaining butter. Pour over the kidneys and serve with the mashed potatoes.

for the kidneys	for 2	for 6	for 20	for 50
lamb kidneys	8	24	80	100
all-purpose (plain) flour	4 tbsp	¾ cup/100 g	2 cups/250 g	5 cups/1.1 kg
English mustard powder	½ tsp	1½ tsp	1½ tbsp	4 tbsp
ground cayenne	½ tsp	1½ tsp	1½ tbsp	4 tbsp
butter	1 tbsp	3 tbsp/40 g	1¼ sticks/5 oz/140 g	3 sticks/¾ lb/350 g
Worcestershire sauce	1 tbsp	3 tbsp	½ cup/120 ml	1¼ cup/300 ml
chicken broth (stock)	½ cup/120 ml	1½ cups/375 ml	4¼ cups/1 L	10½ cups/2.5 L
salt and black pepper	to taste	to taste	to taste	to taste

for the mashed potatoes				
floury potatoes	1 lb/450 g	3 lb/1.25 kg	6 lb/2.5 kg	15 lb/6.2 kg
butter	2 tbsp/25 g	6 tbsp/85 g	1½ sticks/6 oz/180 g	4 sticks/1 lb/450 g
whole (full-fat) milk	scant ½ cup/100 ml	1 cups/250 ml	2 cups/500 ml	5 cups/1.2 L
salt	to taste	to taste	to taste	to taste

Grilled Ox Hearts and Béarnaise Sauce

→ p. 289

1 Trim all the outside fat, membrane, and tubes from the ox hearts so you are left with lean, dense meat. Cut the hearts on the angle into strips about ½-inch (1-cm) thick. Refrigerate until required.

2 For the Béarnaise sauce, put the butter in a small saucepan over medium heat until bubbling. When the bubbling stops, skim the white foam from the top of the melted butter and place in a small bowl and reserve. These are the milk solids.

3 In the meantime, put the white wine vinegar, shallot, peppercorns, and coriander seeds in a small, heavy saucepan. Place over medium-low heat, bring to a simmer, and boil to reduce by half. Pass the reduced liquid through a strainer (sieve) into a small bowl. This is the reduction.

4 Put the egg yolks and half of the reduction in a double boiler over simmering water. Whisk for about 5 minutes until emulsified and foaming. Slowly drizzle in the clarified butter, whisking all the time. The mixture should thicken like mayonnaise. If the mixture is too thick, add a little of the reserved milk solids. Add the chopped herbs and season with the Tabasco, additional reduction, and salt, if needed. Keep warm in the double boiler over lukewarm water.

5 Cook the fries (chips) according to the directions on the package. Season with salt. Keep warm.

6 Heat a ridged grill (griddle pan) or heavy skillet or frying pan with a little oil over medium-high heat. Season the heart strips with salt and black pepper. Cook the ox hearts in a single layer until just seared on all sides but still rare in the middle.

7 Serve immediately with the Béarnaise sauce and fries (chips).

for the Béarnaise sauce	for 2	for 6	for 20	for 50
butter	5 tbsp/75 g	1½ sticks/6 oz/175 g	5 sticks/1¼ lb/500 g	–
white wine vinegar	1 tbsp	2 tbsp	6 tbsp	–
shallot, finely chopped	½	1	3	–
black peppercorns	¼ tsp	½ tsp	1½ tsp	–
coriander seeds	¼ tsp	½ tsp	1½ tsp	–
egg yolks	1	3	9	–
fresh tarragon, finely chopped	2 tsp	2 tbsp	⅓ cup/20 g	–
fresh parsley, finely chopped	2 tsp	2 tbsp	⅓ cup/20 g	–
Tabasco sauce	to taste	to taste	to taste	–

for the ox hearts				
ox hearts	1	3	10	–
balsamic vinegar	2 tbsp	5 tbsp	scant 1 cup/200 ml	–
olive oil	3 tbsp	⅔ cup/150 ml	1 cup/250 ml	–
fresh thyme sprigs	1	1	3	–
garlic cloves, sliced	2	5	1 head	–
salt and black pepper	to taste	to taste	to taste	–

to serve				
frozen fries (chips)	6 oz/175 g	1¼ lb/600 g	4½ lb/2 kg	–
vegetable oil, for frying				–

St. John

← Brett Lemon eating spinach and coconut
daal (opposite).

↑ The antithesis of Michelin-starred dining, before
each service, tables need to be leveled straight on
old wooden floors (top).

↑ Nicole Thompson eating in the bar storage area
(above).

→ Head chef Chris Gillard insists, no matter
how busy, everyone sits down at the table at 11 a.m.
and again at 5 p.m. to dig into some good, old-
fashioned food (overleaf).

St. John

wd~50

Location
New York City, USA

Established
2003

Head chef
Wylie Dufresne

← From left to right: Sam Henderson and John Bignelli. "The most difficult part of shopping at Union Square is getting a taxi." John Bignelli (previous pages).

↑ The team take advantage of a quiet moment to get organized and fold napkins for the diners.

→ Getting the restaurant shipshape and working up an appetite before service.

→ Reggie Soang (overleaf) cooked staff meals for eight months. His favorites were the wd~50 "Big Mac" (p. 303) and Fried Apple Pie (p. 304).

wd~50

wd~50 is one of those rare places where everyone gets to be themselves. So many great chefs have come out of Wylie's kitchen, it's living proof that a free-form approach, combined with a happy culture, works. By now it's such an influential restaurant, not just in New York but around the world, that it's almost become an industry joke: whatever mad thing you think you've come up with, like frying leeks in coffee or serving pig's tails with hazelnuts, they will already have tried it at wd~50.

Here it's all about staff favorites, but a wd~50 version of it. So, although the restaurant style is very entrenched in the American palette, using plenty of sweet, salty, and spicy flavors, Wylie also loves the playfulness that defines Spanish chefs like Ferran Adrià and Andoni Luis Aduriz, especially with things never being quite what they seem. The wd~50 "Big Mac," for example, has been upgraded using proper ground (mince) beef and a sauce that combines house-made ketchup, mayonnaise, and cornichon pickles to create a dish that's reminiscent of the flavor of the original but a hundred times better.

Reggie Soang, who is currently in charge of the staff meal, fuses Taiwanese and American cooking. His take on his mother's recipe for steamed buns is big on flavors that pop: slowly braised and deeply spiced pork side (belly) stuffed into a steamed bun with peanuts, pickled mustard greens, and cilantro (coriander). This kind of dish offers the kind of flavors that make your taste buds sing yet is built on very little. "I don't have a budget for the staff meal," he explains, "but it's fun getting the best out of ingredients for the lowest cost. I'm at the meat station, so I use scraps and bones for flavor, and then go for it with whatever I find in our walk-in."

Fun seems to oil the wd~50 machine, not just in the food but in the whole environment. "When it's time to get down to business, we know how to be serious," says chef de cuisine John Bignelli, "but I think every time you do something difficult you have to find ways to bring levity to the situation." That could be through maintaining a good sense of humor no matter what, or prepping to the beat of a tune you love. "Music is an essential part of making this a great place to work," says Wylie, explaining that they operate a sort of musical democracy in the kitchen. Whoever gets to the iPod dock first gets to play DJ, and the mix of staff from all around the world means there's everything from the jangly mariachi music beloved by the Mexicans when they're scrubbing down the kitchen in the morning to the Portuguese bossa nova that some of the girls bring in. "The only thing I forbid in my kitchen is whistling," Wylie says seriously. "Whistling is the kind of thing you do when you're only half working. It is unacceptable."

Taiwanese Pork Buns

1 Preheat the oven to 300°F/150°C/gas mark 2. Put the spices in a large Dutch oven or casserole dish over low heat and toast, stirring constantly, for 2 minutes until fragrant.

2 Place the pork on top of the spices, then add the rest of the pork ingredients. Cover, bring to a simmer, and transfer to the oven for 3 hours.

3 For the buns, sift the flour, salt, and baking powder into a large bowl. Stir in the sugar, instant dry milk (powdered milk), and yeast. Make a well in the center and add enough warm water to make a soft dough. Knead for 10 minutes. Place in a large, oiled bowl, covered with plastic wrap (clingfilm), and set aside to rise in a warm place for 1 hour.

4 Knead the dough lightly, then divide it into equal pieces for the number of portions you are making. Shape each piece into a ball, then let stand for 5 minutes. Roll the pieces into oval shapes about ¼-inch (5-mm) thick. Brush one side with the oil. Fold the pieces in half and cover with a damp cloth. Let rise for 30 minutes. Steam the buns for 10–12 minutes.

5 Process the peanuts in the food processor until coarsely chopped, then stir in the granulated sugar.

6 Remove the pork from the pan, strain the braising liquid into a saucepan and reserve. Remove the skin and any unwanted fat from the pork. Cut or pull the pork into ¼-inch (5-mm) thick slices. Cover with foil to keep warm.

7 For the sauce, mix the cornstarch (cornflour) with the water. Stir into the strained braising liquid. Slowly bring the mixture to a simmer, stirring frequently. Boil to thicken. Taste and reduce if required. Keep warm.

8 Place each bun on a plate and place a portion of the meat inside each bun. Top with a 4 tbsp ladle of sauce, a spoonful of pickled mustard greens, a tablespoon of ground peanuts, and a few leaves of fresh cilantro (coriander).

for the spices	for 2	for 6	for 20	for 50
whole cloves	–	2 tsp	2 tbsp	5 tbsp
fennel seeds	–	2 tsp	2 tbsp	5 tbsp
whole black peppercorns	–	2 tsp	2 tbsp	5 tbsp
star anise	–	⅓ cup/20 g	1 cup/60 g	2½ cups/150 g
coriander seeds	–	2 tsp	½ cup/30 g	1¼ cups/80 g

for the pork				
whole fresh pork side meat (pork belly)	–	2½ lb/1.2 kg	8 lb/3.6 kg	20 lb/9 kg
dark soy sauce	–	2 cups/500 ml	4 cups/950 ml	10 cups/2.3 L
rice wine vinegar	–	½ cup/120 ml	1 cup/250 ml	2½ cups/650 ml
fresh ginger, sliced	–	2 oz/60 g	3½ oz/100g	9 oz/250 g
garlic, divided and bruised	–	½ head	1 head	2½ heads
brown sugar, packed	–	4 tbsp	½ cup/120 g	1⅓ cups/300 g
water	–	9 cups/2 L	18 cups/4.2 L	9¼ qt/8.7 L
white wine	–	4 tbsp	2 cups/500 ml	5 cups/1.2 L

for the buns				
all-purpose (plain) flour	–	2¾ cups/350 g	8 cups/1 kg	5½ lb/2 .5 kg
salt	–	small pinch	big pinch	1 tbsp

	for 2	for 6	for 20	for 50
superfine (caster) sugar	–	2 tbsp	⅓ cup/70 g	scant 1 cup/175 g
baking powder	–	1½ tsp	2 tsp	5 tsp
instant dry milk (powdered milk)	–	2 tsp	2 tbsp	5 tbsp
active dry (fast-action) yeast	–	1½ tsp	5 tsp	4 tbsp
warm water	–	scant 1 cup/200 ml	2¼ cups/575 ml	5¾ cups/1.3 L
vegetable oil, for brushing	–	1 tbsp	2 tbsp	5 tbsp
for the sauce				
braising liquid from pork	–			
cornstarch (cornflour)	–	4 tbsp	⅔ cup/75 g	1⅔ cups/200 g
water	–	⅔ cup/150 ml	scant 2 cups/450 ml	4½ cups/1.1 L
to serve				
salted, toasted peanuts	–	⅔ cup/120 g	2 cups/250 g	5 cups/675 g
granulated sugar	–	4 tbsp/60 g	¾ cup + 2 tbsp/175 g	2 cups/400 g
Chinese pickled mustard greens, coarsely chopped	–	4 oz/120 g	8 oz/225 g	1¼ lb/675 g
fresh cilantro (coriander) leaves	–	4 tbsp	1 cup/40 g	2½ cups/100 g

wd~50 "Big Mac"

→ p. 300

1 First make the sauce. Mix together all of the ingredients. Season to taste with salt. Cover and place in the refrigerator until required.

2 To make the burgers, put the oil in a skillet or frying pan and stir in the onions. Cook over medium-low heat, stirring occasionally, until soft and translucent. Turn the heat to medium and continue to cook until golden brown. Set aside.

3 Knead the meat lightly with clean hands until soft enough to form patties. Divide into double the number of burgers required, about ½-inch (1-cm) thick. Place on a tray layered with parchment paper. Cover with plastic wrap (clingfilm) and refrigerate until ready to cook.

4 Cook the burgers on a barbecue or under the broiler (grill) for 1½ minutes per side for medium rare, 2 minutes per side for medium, or 4 minutes per side for well done.

5 Melt the cheese over the patties.

6 Spread the sauce on both sides of the buns. Place the lettuce and dill pickles on the bottom half of the buns, then flip the burger over so it is cheese side down. Top with the caramelized onions, the second burger, and the bun top.

for the sauce	for 2	for 6	for 20	for 50
mayonnaise	5 tbsp	scant 1 cup/200 g	3 cups/665 g	–
ketchup	2 tbsp	5 tbsp	1 cup/250 ml	–
cornichons, finely chopped	2 tbsp	⅔ cup/120 g	2 cups/400 g	–
white vinegar	1 tbsp	3 tbsp	½ cup/120 ml	–
onion powder	½ tsp	2 tsp	2 tbsp	–
garlic powder	½ tsp	2 tsp	2 tbsp	–
salt	to taste	to taste	to taste	–
for the burgers				
vegetable oil	2 tsp	1 tbsp	1¼ cups/300 ml	–
yellow onions, finely chopped	½ medium	1 medium	3 medium	–
ground (mince) beef	1 lb/450 g	3 lb/1.35 kg	10 lb/4.5 kg	–
American cheese slices	4	12	40	–
sesame burger buns	2	6	20	–
iceburg lettuce, thinly sliced	¼ head	½ head	1½ heads	–
sliced dill pickles (gherkins)	5 tbsp	1⅓ cups/200 g	4 cups/575 g	–

Fried Apple Pie

1   First make the dough (pastry). Sift the flour and salt into a large bowl.

2   Cut the butter into ½-inch (1-cm) cubes and toss in the flour. Squeeze the butter into the flour. Make sure the butter is well coated with flour and the lumps are no larger than peas.

3   Drizzle the water over the flour and incorporate with your fingers to form a dough.

4   Gently knead the dough until smooth, and flatten into portions (two for the six-person quantity. Wrap in plastic wrap (clingfilm) and refrigerate for 1 hour.

5   Meanwhile, make the filling. Put the butter into a noncorrosive saucepan over medium heat. Heat until the butter turns medium brown, then add the remaining ingredients. Cook, stirring occasionally, until the apples break down and the filling becomes syrupy. Turn onto a cold plate or trays and let cool to room temperature.

6   Roll out the dough in circles, one at a time to ⅛-inch (25-mm) thick on a lightly floured surface. Cut into strips about 3 inches (8 cm) wide.

7   Place 1 tbsp of filling on half of the pastry placed 2 inches (5 cm) apart. Brush the pastry edges with a little cold water, then cover with a second strip of pastry and press around each mound of filling to seal, like making raviolis. Try not to trap air inside the pastries. Cut into individual pies and seal the edges by pressing with the tines of a fork. Place in a single layer on a baking sheet. Refrigerate until the pastry is firm.

8   Heat 2 inches (5 cm) vegetable oil in a large saucepan or heat the oil in a deep fryer to 375°F/190°C.

9   Carefully place a few of the pies into the oil, being careful not to let the oil splash on your skin. Fry for 3 minutes or until golden brown.

10 Carefully remove each pie from the oil with a slotted spoon and place on a tray lined with paper towels. Sprinkle with a light dusting of extra fine (caster) sugar. Cool for a short time before eating as the filling will be very hot.

for the dough (pastry)	for 2	for 6	for 20	for 50
all-purpose (plain) flour	–	2 cups/250 g	6 cups/750 g	15 cups/1.9 kg
salt	–	⅔ tsp	2 tsp	5 tsp
butter	–	1½ sticks/6 oz/175 g	4 sticks/1 lb/450 g	2½ lb/1.1 kg
ice water (approximately)	–	3 tbsp	½ cup/120 ml	1¼ cups/300 ml

for the filling	for 2	for 6	for 20	for 50
butter	–	2 tsp	2 tbsp	5 tbsp
apples, peeled, cored, and diced	–	1	3	8
granulated sugar	—	3 tbsp	⅔ cup/125 g	1½ cups/300 g
lemon juice	–	⅓ lemon	1 lemon	2–3 lemons
water	–	1 tbsp	4 tbsp	⅔ cup/150 ml
ground cinnamon	–	¼ tsp	1 tsp	2½ tsp
ground nutmeg	–	pinch	½ tsp	1¼ tsp
all-purpose (plain) flour	–	3 tbsp	⅓ cup/50 g	1 cup/125 g

↑ The best things come in small packages:
Taiwanese Pork Buns (p. 302).

↑ Beneath a large skylight the staff meal buffet starts to take shape.

→ An afternoon pick-me-up: the cultish "wd~50 Gulp" and cookies.

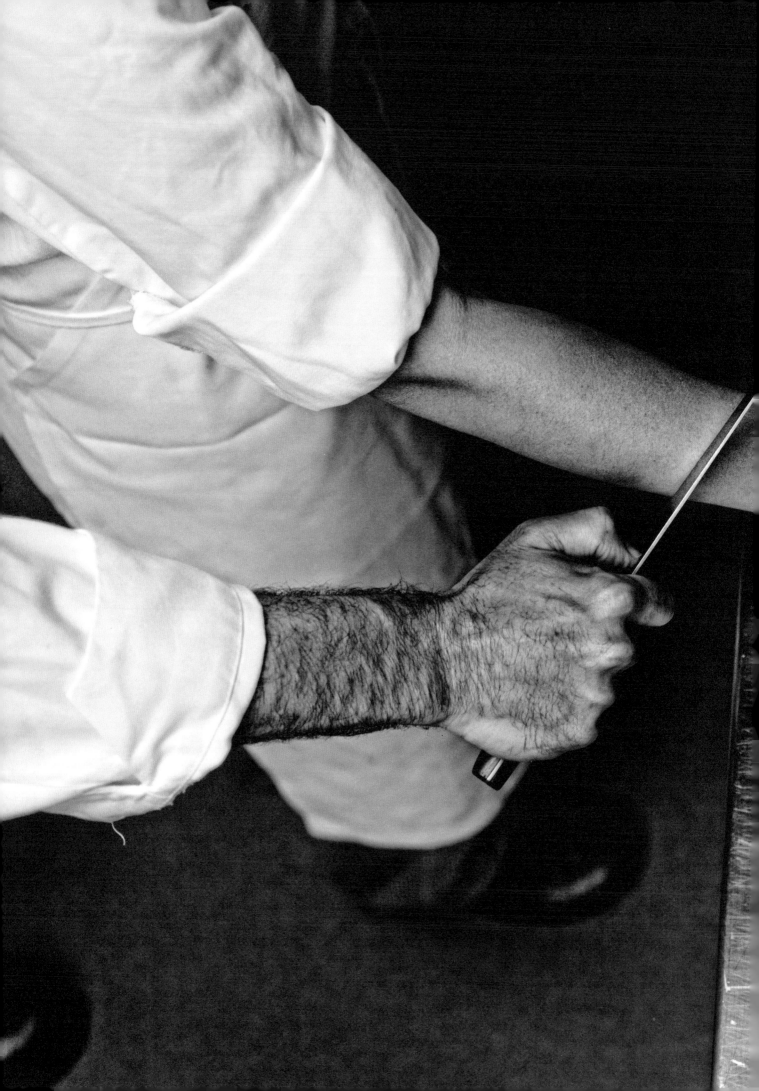

Index

Thanks to all the chefs that opened up their
restaurants and kitchens, allowing us to roam
freely. And to all the staff that keeps this industry
running. This book is for you.

Phaidon Press Limited
Regent's Wharf
All Saints Street
London, N1 9PA

Phaidon Press Inc.
65 Bleecker Street
New York, NY 10012

www.phaidon.com

First published 2014
© 2014 Phaidon Press Limited

ISBN 978 0 7148 6581 2

A CIP catalogue record for this book is
available from the British Library

Photography: Per-Anders Jörgensen
Idea, concept and research:
Per-Anders Jörgensen and Lotta Jörgensen
Texts and captions: Tara Stevens

Commissioning editor: Emilia Terragni
Project editor: Daniel Hurst
Production controller: Rebecca Price

Printed in China

Notes on the recipes

Cooking times are for guidance only. If using
a fan (convection) oven, follow the manufacturer's
instructions concerning the oven temperatures.

Eggs are medium (US large) size, unless specified.
Some recipes include lightly cooked eggs, meat
and fish. These should be avoided by the elderly,
infants, pregnant women, convalescents and anyone
with an impaired immune system.

Exercise a very high level of caution when following
recipes involving any potentially hazardous activity,
including the use of high temperatures, open flames
and when deep-frying. In particular, when deep frying
add food carefully to avoid splashing, wear long
sleeves and never leave the pan unattended.

Mushrooms should be wiped clean.

All spoon measurements are level.
1 teaspoon = 5ml. 1 tablespoon = 15ml.
Australian standard tablespoons are 20ml;
Australian readers are advised to use 3 teaspoons
in place of 1 tablespoon.